HISTORIES

SHAKESPEARE'S

Ten Epic Plays *at a Breakneck Pace!*

HISTORIES

SHAKESPEARE'S

Ten Epic Plays *at a Breakneck Pace!*

Recklessly sliced from the Historical Plays of William Shakespeare
Adapted, Edited, and Explained...

by Timothy Mooney

Shakespeare's Histories
© 2013 by Timothy Mooney

Credits:
Cover Illustration by Lee Rushton
Map Designs by Lee Rushton

ISBN 13: 978-0-9831812-4-8
ISBN 10: 0983181241

Advance Response to…
Shakespeare's Histories
Ten Epic Plays at a Breakneck Pace

Palpable *and* delicious! Accessible and immensely enjoyable, Mooney shows how Shakespeare the playwright was able to blend regency with the universality of the human condition. The implications for lesson plans and cross-disciplines of drama, speech, and English departments are limitless. ***Shakespeare's Histories*** is versatile enough for performance at a fringe festival or a cafetorium, and could be housed within a high school English class or a university library. For the novice performer or the well-informed scholar, a must-read/must-own addition to any collection of Shakespeare studies.
> *Aaron Adair, Ph.D., Assistant Dean, Southeastern Oklahoma University*

A really excellent distillation of very complex history… Would make a great companion piece to any season that's doing one of the histories… [The speeches] are compelling, and really do make you want to read the plays themselves!
> *Christina Gutierrez, Producing Artistic Director, 7 Towers Theatre*

"Shakespeare's Histories" is an absolutely wonderful new approach to an old subject which is often greeted by students with a groan. Having a degree in Theatre and English and attended RADA, I now teach at university level and will certainly be incorporating this in any Shakespeare or Dramatic Literature class I'll be teaching. I'm sure my students' enthusiasm will equal my own. Mooney's work is a delight even to those already familiar with the material.
> *Melissa Berry, Mount St. Mary's College, Los Angeles*

Brilliant, funny and inspiring.
> *Marshall James Smith II, Attorney*

The audience was immediately engaged and enthralled. Mooney managed to illuminate not only major events such as the War of the Roses or the Hundred Years' War, but also nuances of character. Even in the midst of horrific acts of slaughter and revenge killings, Mooney manages to draw laughs with ironic understatement… The ongoing humor underlines the grotesqueness of it all, and makes it memorable. ***Shakespeare's Histories*** left the audience with a clear sense of the events that forged the timeline of the history of England with humor, narrative, visual images and breathless enthusiasm.
> *Maureen McHugh, Claiborne Clarion*

Tim Mooney's brilliant, thoughtful, stripped-down histories is a gift to all performers of classical texts who want to stretch themselves and thrill their audiences.
> *John D. Huston (Actor)*

ABOUT THE ADAPTOR/EDITOR/EXPLAINER:

Timothy Mooney has adapted seventeen of Molière's plays to the stage, seen in the United States, Canada, Scotland, Italy, Indonesia and India, with many of them published by Playscripts, Inc. His one-man plays, *Molière than Thou* and *Lot o' Shakespeare* are turning a new generation on to Molière and Shakespeare, and his latest, *The Greatest Speech of All Time*, recreates actual historical speeches ranging from Socrates to Martin Luther King Jr. As Artistic Director of the Stage Two Theatre, Tim produced nearly fifty plays in five years. He taught acting at Northern Illinois University, and published his own newsletter. *The Script Review*. Tim inaugurated the *TMRT Press*, with his long-awaited acting text, *Acting at the Speed of Life; Conquering Theatrical Style* in 2011, followed by *The Big Book of Molière Monologues* in 2012. In 2013, Tim began releasing parts of his one-man catalogue into published form, beginning with *Molière Than Thou* and *Criteria, a One-Man Comic Sci-Fi Thriller!*

SPECIAL THANKS:

To Isaac Asimov, Brother Robert Ruhl, Mary Lamb, Joe Proctor, Charley Antalosky, Kermit Brown, Bruce Cromer, James Donadio, John Frederick Jones, Judy Langford, Martin Platt... great Shakespearean thinkers and actors who shaped my understanding of all of this.

From the Adaptor/Editor/Explainer...

Here's my take on how we feel about Shakespeare:

We love, love, love his Comedies...

We are profoundly touched and moved by his Tragedies...

His Histories, we're not so sure about.

Oh, sure, Henry V, and Richard III, and maybe Henry IV, Part 1, those are pretty good...

But the seven other History plays? Not so much.

For his Comedies, Shakespeare's "batting average" is probably up in the eighty-percent range, amongst those plays we would gladly go to see.

For his Tragedies? Maybe seventy percent.

His Histories?

Thirty percent.

If Shakespeare were a basketball player with a free-throw average of seventy-to-eighty percent, a sudden drop to thirty would be a sign of some horrible injury!

Of course we can examine exactly when these plays were written and notice that many of them emerged early in the career of this great playwright, so maybe that accounts for something.

But take a look at some of the amazing lines in these plays! Each play carries speeches of breathtaking profundity, amazing insight into life, death and, in this case, the challenges and perils of monarchy: speeches that stand confidently alongside the dialogue in any of Shakespeare's other works.

So perhaps the difference lies in us!

Shakespeare, writing in the 1590s, was describing events dating back as far as 1300, but mostly those key events dating from 1400-1533. In other words, the bulk of the action of these works predated Shakespeare's audience by 70-200 years.

Those same events predate *our* lives from *480-610 years!*

The average American school-child can fairly easily describe a handful of events from 235 years ago (the Revolutionary War) and can probably give you thumbnail descriptions of some of the characters in that drama: George Washington, Thomas Jefferson, John Adams, Benjamin Franklin… They probably even have a good sense of what those folks looked like!

Seventy years ago we were in the thick of the Second World War. With how many events and "characters" are we familiar, spanning the time from the Revolutionary War to the Second World War? How many events and people can we name without even logging on to the internet?

If I told a story about George Washington that somehow involved a Cherry Tree, that "Cherry Tree" would have resonance for ninety percent of any Americans who heard the story, whether or not George Washington ever chopped it down, or told any form of a truth or lie with regard to that tree.

If Benjamin Franklin alluded to flying a kite…

If Abraham Lincoln referred to a number as being several "score"…

If General Custer talked about Native American issues…

If Franklin Roosevelt talked about Social Security… or "fear, itself…"

In other words, Shakespeare's audience came to these plays already armed with a significant sense of who these characters were, what they stood for, and what they did, and how some of those things got done. Also, growing up with a much stronger "oral tradition," stories about history were passed down from one generation to the next, without the vast distractions that television or the internet would have introduced into the lexicon of stories that might have surrounded them. What they had was a tight, coherent narrative, upon which their story-tellers, playwrights, and jesters might embroider or improvise at any given moment.

In other words, these History plays, which currently live in our own experience with a batting average of thirty percent (only the most daring Shakespeare festivals risk their box office success by producing them) are quite likely much better than we give them credit for. We simply aren't coming to the table armed with such a ready index of information about the characters and plots that are being spun in our direction.

If only we came equipped with the same background or frame of mind that Shakespeare's Elizabethan audience already possessed... it might well open up a whole new set of Shakespearean plays to our dramatic lexicon. Might it at least reinvigorate Shakespeare's free-throw average?

What if we arrived at the table with the sensibility enabling us to appreciate Shakespeare's Histories with the same ready knowledge that he provides in the self-contained plots of his Comedies and his Tragedies?

What if we simply knew the difference between Richard (the Lion Heart) Richard II and Richard III?

What if we knew one Henry from another?

What if we knew what the hell happened between the triumph of Henry V and the horrors of Henry VI?

What if we simply had a sense of the overall arc of the story that we were following?

Well then we might be able to sit back and enjoy the great embroidery... those embellishments which enrich Shakespeare's great speeches.

We might, as in any horror story, want to cry out to the characters: "No, no! Go the other way!"

As many in Shakespeare's audience surely did.

How to Read This

My goal, here, is to fill you up with as much of that necessary information as I can through the course of a single hour... okay, maybe seventy-five minutes.

That is to say: one hour of playing time! Performed full-out, this material can be expressed in sixty minutes upon the stage... by actors who are willing to commit to picking up their cues,[1] or even overlap their dialogue, led by a Narrator who rips into the words with all the excitement of a great sportscaster.

I cannot attest to how much "reading time" this material may take. But if you want to get a sense of the action moving forward: *stick to the right-hand pages!*

The script, you will immediately discover, is on the right-hand side of these pages, while the left-hand side is splashed with notes interspersed almost throughout. I'm guessing that most of you, reading this for the first time, will ignore most of the notes and read the script straight through. And, I'm also guessing that some of the photos and charts will catch your eye in

---

[1] See my book, *Acting at the Speed of Life; Conquering Theatrical Style* for more input on a suggested style of performance for Shakespeare and classical theatre.

the process, and you won't be able to resist glancing their way from time to time. (I've also included the original First Folio titles, for fun.)

Most of the portraits are of unknown origin, but probably date from the late-16th to the early-17th century. The artist(s) would have had no actual contact with the subjects, and may simply be improving upon crude drawings of those kings. And yet, a visual impression helps us to separate one Henry or one Richard from another in our minds. Anchoring a personality around an image lessens our dependency on the sometimes inconspicuous distinction that some very similar Roman Numerals provide.

Regardless, we may be sure that this will read much faster than the original, which, collectively, adds up to about thirty hours of stage time!

My intent is to create a baseline understanding of the narrative thread that holds these plays together: to give the reader/audience a clear vision of how Shakespeare's audience might have received it, with a minimal investment of research time.

In doing so, this book hopes to make those other "twenty-nine hours" more productive for the reader/viewer. With all of the names, locations, battles and political strategies that hold these plays together, that tenuous through-line is very easy to lose, and once it is lost, the vague sense of "feeling overwhelmed" makes it pretty hard to claw our way back to understanding or appreciation.

Shakespeare may have had no idea that someone hundreds of years into the future might be reading this. Or that, if they were, they would need to know what in the world happened to Henry V, or why Joan of Arc is not a glorious heroine, or why Edward III and John of Gaunt turned out to be such crucial lynchpins in the Plantagenet family tree, or just how awful Queen Margaret turned out to be.

He also might not realize that you don't already know that one of the Henrys goes mad, and that the Duke of Gloucester becomes Richard III.

Which is why he *doesn't explain these things!*

Besides which, there were plenty of things that Shakespeare simply outright **hides from us** because saying the thing aloud would have gotten him into lots of trouble!

That's a whole lot of information that you need to know, and I'm hoping to trick your brain into absorbing it.

The Tone
That is at least part of the reason for the irreverence of my tone through this play. If I were to say that "The Duke of Suffolk felt an attraction to Margaret of Anjou, and wanted to keep her nearby, even though, as a married man, he was unable to marry her himself, which led to encouraging King Henry to marry her…" you probably have one kind of reaction.

But if I tell you that Suffolk decided to "pimp her out to King Henry instead…" you have another kind of reaction. I'm guessing that this different way of looking at this tangle of relationships will wedge its way into your head a little more vividly. Of course, I am counting on you, dear reader/viewer, having somewhat cosmopolitan tastes. (I am also making an educated guess that this is *exactly* the frame of mind through which the Elizabethan audience would have viewed this particular transaction.)

I offer what I intend to be a humorous perspective on material that we assume is dry, dry, dry… and I include the occasional Shakespearean line that sounds ridiculously offensive, and we gasp and chortle and question whether Shakespeare had any idea what he was writing (i.e., Henry V talking about tennis balls, or our realization that the nickname for "Richard" was, back then, what it remains today)!

Embracing my Ignorance
I have always been averse to studying history, but have found myself, again and again, diving in up to my eyeballs trying to make sense of these plays that I didn't understand.

The best thing that I have to offer an audience is my ignorance.

I tend to notice when I don't know something. And, I have a good guess for when the average person will be left, along with me, in the dark.

I notice when a lot of characters have the same name.

I notice when characters who were once called one name, are later called by another name.

I notice when something seems somehow "off," with no explanation provided.

And I also notice how much easier it is to absorb information when somebody alerts me that this thing that's coming up is confusing… or mocks the very nature of the confusion surrounding it.

The more that I explore these plays, the more that I notice that they make the most sense when you discover them in chronological order. Just about all of these people are connected, and a lot of them appear in multiple plays. If I study Henry V, and then double back to Richard II, and then jump forward to Richard III, I'm reading lots of great material, but none of the story lines strike me as being linked in any way, and I am outrageously clueless about how much these historical actions intersected.

My guesses about these plays' several time frames might have varied by some 400 years! Again and again, I have had to drop one book and pick up another, just to check what dates all of these things happened. (I try to place those relevant dates under your nose, more or less at the moment you might be wondering about them. Of course Shakespeare, telling the story in his own sometimes-invented chronology, is not always helping.) I could never remember which Richard was *not* the hunchback! And I kept waiting for Henry VI to assert himself and be every bit as much the leader as his father was… as, I suppose, the English people also did, back then…

My History with Shakespeare

I started studying Shakespeare in high school, and I have long credited *Thor* comic books with making the whole archaic "thee" and "thou" style of speech seem natural to me. Brother Ruhl, at St. Viator High School was one of the most challenging teachers I've ever had, and you really had to come to class with your wits sharpened when facing his critical inquiry. A theatre major in college, I took Shakespeare in two separate English classes and in acting class. I followed this up with a summer internship at the Alabama Shakespeare Festival, where I got to see some terrific actors who really shaped the lens through which I saw these plays.

From there it was on to grad school to study directing (exploring the Marowitz *Measure for Measure*) and internships with the Milwaukee Rep (working on *Macbeth*) and the Seattle Rep (assistant directing *Tartuffe*). From there it was on to a ton of work with brand new plays in manuscript form, editing *The Script Review* and running the Stage Two Theatre Company as its Artistic Director for almost five years.

One day Stage Two decided to produce Molière, and I ventured to write a version of *Tartuffe*. I was combining my knowledge of Shakespearean language with my remembrance of that previous *Tartuffe,* placing dialogue into the imagined mouths of the very talented actors I remembered… in rhymed iambic pentameter…

Tartuffe led to a new career as a writer/adaptor of Molière scripts, which led me back to being an actor, as I got to play many of the roles that Molière himself played, way back when. My parallel existence to Molière led me to a one-man show, *Molière than Thou*, which I have now been performing on the road for almost thirteen years! Somewhere in there, I evolved into a one-man repertory theatre, and found myself revisiting all of the Shakespeare plays, memorizing one monologue from each of them!

But while *Lot o' Shakespeare* was a random event (I determined performance order by way of a spinning bingo cage), I was aware that, isolated, the History portions would actually make more sense in chronological order.

I found myself in a conversation with a professor who was going to produce a Shakespeare play as part of a broader, university-wide study of English culture, and we pondered which Shakespeare plays might most effectively stress particularly English themes.

Of course, the tragedies and the comedies are mostly set in foreign countries (with the exception of King Lear, which is set in medieval England). But then there were the histories…

And there, we noticed the question that all Shakespeare producers must face at one point or another: Are we really limited to a repertory of just three workable Shakespeare histories?

I found myself inspired to work on a draft of *The Henriad*: a work which combined *Richard II, Henry IV Parts 1 & 2* and *Henry V* into a single evening's performance. And then I started looking at *The War of the Roses*, trimming *Henry VI, 1, 2 & 3* and *Richard III* into a single four-hour event...

As these plays started to "connect" in my mind, I started to think: "What if I were to perform all of my history monologues in order...?" And "What if I added, say, another monologue from each of the plays to fill out an hour-long introduction to these works?"

Shakespeare's Histories began to take shape. I started to notice themes popping up, and to notice how some speeches fed the narrative better than others. As much as I loved Talbot's speech before the gates of Orleans (and as much effort as I'd put into memorizing the thing), it wasn't really feeding the story line. Even some of the astonishing lines of Richard III (in his early incarnation as Gloucester from *Henry VI, Part 3*) had to go!

And with each pass through, I began to notice the plot mechanisms that set up some of the most famous twists!

King Henry's insomnia makes sense when Hal's big mistake is assuming that his father, *who can't sleep*, has died.

The White Rose and the Red Rose make sense when we consider that these English lords who think that they should be king are *unable to say so aloud* (at risk of committing treason). And so, they let "dumb significants" speak for them.

The more I would cut, the more I would notice the thing bonding into one collective, interdependent story! These things were always *meant* to be part of a larger tale: English history writ large, in ten interconnected chunks!

The Great Themes
In order to know what to cut, I had to somehow know what to keep. I was responsible for the prism through which this material would be viewed. With much gratitude to Isaac Asimov, whose brilliant and out-of-print *Asimov's Guide to Shakespeare* is my favorite resource, I have found these plays make absolute sense when seen in light of ongoing issues of royal succession that run through all ten scripts.

Shakespeare, himself, never comes out and says this. (Of course, we have no commentary from him about *any* of his works.) But his audience clearly understands that, in the well-ordered universe of Elizabethan society, we move from Gods to Archangels to Angels, on down the line to humans, and at the top of *that* pile is The King. ("Kings are Earth's Gods," notes Pericles.) And decisions about who gets to rule, and when, are decided by divine intervention. After all, God decides who gets born, to whom, and in what particular order, which thereby determines who gets to rule.

In short, what you need to know about the rules are: the monarchy passes from the king to the king's eldest son. If that eldest son has a son, then that grandson is next in line to be king, no matter how much more mature, capable or talented the second, third, fourth or fifth son of the previous king might be. Only when a first son dies without any heir can we look to another son to take over. And these rules are scrupulously enforced!

Except on those occasions in which they are not.

And when little man jumps the barrier of that divinely maintained queue, *bad things happen!*

The more we look at them, the more we realize that these plays are riddled with issues of succession, and I did my best to feature those particular speeches and scenes where issues of succession are being questioned or resolved, either overtly or indirectly.

Inherent Sexism

There is no way around this: These plays are inherently sexist. But they are only sexist to the extent that Elizabethan society was sexist. (Elizabeth, herself, was the exception and not the rule.) The plays are about succession, and the first rule of succession is that *Male Heirs are what Matter!*

(Okay, the FIRST rule of succession is actually: "Don't talk about succession!")

I'm not here to "fix" Elizabethan social norms. Women were not allowed to perform on stage. They weren't allowed to write plays,[2] nor were they allowed to inherit. The reason that Elizabeth Woodville came to the court in *Henry VI, Part 3* (where she met Edward IV) was because she was strictly proscribed from inheriting her late-husband's estate. She had to get special dispensation from the king to keep her family possessions.

In spite of that, Shakespeare stands independent of his contemporaries, writing more and better roles for women into his plays. A comparison of Shakespeare's characters with those characters depicted in his play's original source materials (described in "*Sweet Swan,*" noted below), show a striking improvement for women in Shakespeare's plays.

I have no agenda to generate more female stage time as some sort of post-modern compensation… I'm on a tight schedule as it is. Boiling all of this down to a play that is about the whole succession process forces us to feature the men in these plays even more exclusively.

---

[2] For a real eye-opener, read *Sweet Swan of Avon; Did a Woman Write Shakespeare?* by Robin P. Williams.

Fortunately, we are growing much more accepting of cross-gender casting, and, however gradually, we are learning to look beyond physical characteristics to appreciate the psychological traits and attitudes that make a given actor "right" for a role.

(In other words, I'm totally okay with casting women as the men… or the Narrator… As far as I'm concerned, this might just as well be a one-*woman* show. But don't freak out when I take on Joan of Arc!)

The King as Human
The next favorite-ist theme of Shakespeare is a close parallel (or perhaps a perpendicular) to these themes of succession. In spite of the fact that God is the deciding power in choosing the King, the King, himself, is still a human being… with all of the wants, needs, desires, foibles, temptations and failings that a human being has.

And while we assume that a king might never want for anything, reality is always a major come-down, and the crown, itself, never solves the problem. Shakespeare never tires of pointing this out, and this theme manifests in some of the most soaring lyrical passages, such as:

"Cover your heads and mock not flesh and blood
With solemn reverence: throw away respect,
Tradition, form and ceremonious duty,
For you have but mistook me all this while:
I live with bread like you, feel want,
Taste grief, need friends: subjected thus,
How can you say to me, I am a king?"
(*Richard II, Act III, Scene 2*)

"Cans't thou, O partial sleep, give thy repose
To the wet sea-boy in an hour so rude,
And in the calmest and most stillest night,
With all appliances and means to boot,
Deny it to a king? Then happy low, lie down!
Uneasy lies the head that wears a crown."
(*Henry IV, Part 2, Act III, Scene 1*)

"I think the king is but a man, as I am: the violet smells to him as it doth to me: the element shows to him as it doth to me; all his senses have but human conditions: his ceremonies laid by, in his nakedness he appears but a man; and though his affections are higher mounted than ours, yet, when they stoop, they stoop with the like wing."
(*Henry V, Act IV, Scene 1*)

"O God! Methinks it were a happy life
To be no better then a homely swain…"
(*Henry VI, Part 3, Act II, Scene 5*)

Errata

In the course of squeezing all of this history into a single hour, there are portions of the story that do not fit the through line of the narrative. I will attempt to flesh out the story (and correct the record) when convenient, in the opposing pages.

Occasionally, it will be Shakespeare, himself, who has taken the shortcut. At the risk of disturbing his old bones, I will point that out from time to time, too.

And, there are places where Shakespeare simply mis-tells the story. Occasionally, he will say things that are deliberately misleading, sometimes in the interest of streamlining the narrative, such as combining the Edmund Mortimers or the Beauforts[3] into single characters, or perhaps he is avoiding offending Queen Elizabeth. If Shakespeare's effort was to streamline things, then my one-hour summary of the multitude of plot threads dares not re-tangle that knot by attempting to explain or re-right that wrong.

But if, from time to time, there is an opportunity to point out a suspect narrative choice (such as the amazing success rate of any prophecies uttered), then it strikes me as a fun bit of perspective to share. And, I think that Shakespeare still holds up well under occasional snide commentary.

The Big Why

I am reminded of a probably-apocryphal story of the woman who went to see *Hamlet* for the first time. Interviewed on her way out of the theatre, she reportedly said: "I don't see what the big deal is. He just strung a bunch of famous quotes together."

I suspect that the typical response to *Shakespeare's Histories* will be fairly similar. Every time I revisit this text I am reminded of all of those great lines that I somehow knew already, without ever knowing from whence they came.

I think that this exploration makes a good jumping-on place for the enjoyment of a series of plays that are clearly underrepresented in our theatrical repertory.

If the vast body of high school and college students had easier access to the pool of knowledge and understanding that lies behind these, then perhaps these plays would not seem like such a daunting, impossible wall to scale.

Perhaps the chance to crack open our "Collected Works" to these largely undisturbed pages might seem more of an invigorating opportunity than what it seems now: a discombobulating, narcotizing fog.

---

[3] The "Beauforts" don't actually fit into this retelling of the tale, so don't worry: you haven't overlooked them.

Perhaps attendance numbers for our theatres might not drop off so severely when "Histories" are on the bill.

Moreover, perhaps the lessons of these plays: the political lessons, the mistakes that we humans make from one generation to the next, never seeming to learn… perhaps we might see one or two of those coming.

There is a moment in the tide of these historical events in which Shakespeare captures the end of chivalry as he knows it: Sir John Talbot's son dies, pure in the belief of standing for something larger than himself, even as the political players shift to treachery and narcicism, with individuals and parties placing their own interests over the good of the country. This shifting tide clearly ebbs and flows in its shift between individual self-interest and altruism.

Within living memory, we Americans found our country calling us to "Ask not what your country can do for you, ask what you can do for your country." And within more recent memory, we find that same country choosing shut-down and default amid fits of political pique.

When I read or see Jack Cade, railing against education, and arguing in favor of ignorance… I hear today's echoes of distrust for science, feeding the general public with ignorance, confusion and superstition.

When Henry Bolingbroke grabs the crown to himself, simply because it was within his reach… I see every tin-pot dictator from the third world on up to the first.

When Richard III lies and kills and cheats his way to the top (while the public stands aghast and silent)… I see every Machievellian politician, lying with impunity, before a media too embarrassed and cowed to point out that the policies endorsed will do more harm than good.

The lessons of these plays are healthy things for us to hear, and we are liberated by the thoughts and the perspectives that Shakespeare shares.

I want to bring those lessons back within our reach. And I want them to be fun.

Break a leg!

Tim

Cast of Characters

Play	Characters
	Narrator
King John	King John
Richard II	Richard II Bishop of Carlisle
Henry IV (2 Plays)	Falstaff Prince Hal (Henry V) Hotspur Henry IV
Henry V	Chorus Henry V (Prince Hal) Dauphin Princess Katherine (*Single line*)
Henry VI (3 Plays)	York Talbot Joan La Pucelle (Joan of Arc) Jack Cade Henry VI Richard of Gloucester (Richard III) Prince Edward Edward IV (*Single line*) Clarence/George (*Single line*)
Richard III	Richard of Gloucester / Richard III Lady Anne Queen Elizabeth
Henry VIII	Henry VIII Cranmer, Archbishop of Canterbury

Time: 1066-1533

Place: England and France

TIMOTHY MOONEY

Production Notes

At first, at lease, I wrote this to be performed as a one-man play… as a demanding virtuoso performance over sixty breathless minutes of recitation.

But the more that I wrote it the more I realized that it could be performed in a vast array of styles and manners, with a wide range of casts: from one, to two, three, all the way up to twenty-five.

The narration could be managed by a single actor who might become the enthusiastic glue that holds this play together, or it might be shared amongst an ensemble who could take over the narration: in turn, unified or overlapping, reader's theatre style.

It can be performed in period costumes, or in modern dress.

The actors could change whole costumes, or, perhaps just crowns and other headgear.

It can be performed on an empty stage, or on a set.

The producer might replicate some of the photos and family trees included in this text to project as slides, and give visual reinforcement to the issues of succession that drive the action.

Do I have particular demands?

I'd really like to see it done in an hour. (It can be done! I've done it!) But 75 minutes is plenty fast. If you want to, you could integrate some of the trimmed speeches (included on the left-hand pages) back to their full length to go a little longer (and you could take an intermission after Henry V, if you were looking to make a full evening out of it), but beware! Part of what makes this work is the *through line of action*, and if you unravel that thread too much, we may start to lose our sense of how all this links up… or we may need to change the subtitle!

William the Conqueror

Descendants of William the Conqueror
(Not all relations included)

MONARCHS
Of England
(Dates of Reign)

WILLIAM I
(The Conqueror)
(1066–1087)

WILLIAM II
(1087–1100)

HENRY I
(1100–1135)

Henry I

Geoffrey of Anjou
(Plantagenet)

Empress Matilda
(April, 1141-
November, 1141)

HENRY II
(Plantagenet)
(1154–1189)

Henry II

King Stephen, Grandson to William I (through his daughter, Adela), also ruled between the reigns of Henry I and Henry II, and Geoffrey of Anjou was never, himself, king.

Empress Matilda, had a disputed seven-month reign, in the middle of Stephen's rule. She was never crowned.

The Angevin Empire

4

PRELUDE
(1066-1199)

NARRATOR[4]

The year: 1066! The Normans Conquest over England, led by William the Conqueror.

William begets William II and Henry I, who becomes father-in-law to Geoffrey of Anjou, the first known as a "Plantagenet."

Geoffrey fathers Henry II, who becomes king of shortly after marrying Eleanor of Aquitaine, thus creating the Angevin Empire, a territory encompassing not only England, but most of France as well.

Henry is father to five sons. The most popular, "Richard the Lion-Heart," reigns from 1189 to 1199. When Richard dies in 1199 without an heir, succession might have gone one of two ways. It could have gone to Arthur, the 3-year-old son of Henry's fourth son. Or, it could pass directly to Henry's fifth, and only surviving son, John.

This is the central issue in all of Shakespeare's History Plays: Succession. In each instance, a good, clean, undisputed succession leads to happiness and prosperity. An uncertain, contentious succession leads to dispute, dissent and rebellion. Given that Shakespeare's own monarch (the childless Queen Elizabeth), was now in her sixties, an ancient age at that time, Shakespeare was essentially telling horror stories about the dangers a disputed succession might bring to England of the seventeenth century.

---

[4] The "Narrator" is actually the lead character in this play, and will frame our view of every scene we encounter. We may assume that all the material bridging the Shakespearean passages (written in prose and italicized) represents our faithful "Narrator," stepping in to guide us. I cannot understate the importance of the energy and excitement that the Narrator needs to generate. He's like a great sportscaster, striving to describe, with some wry humor, the astonishing highlights of a hotly contested battle.

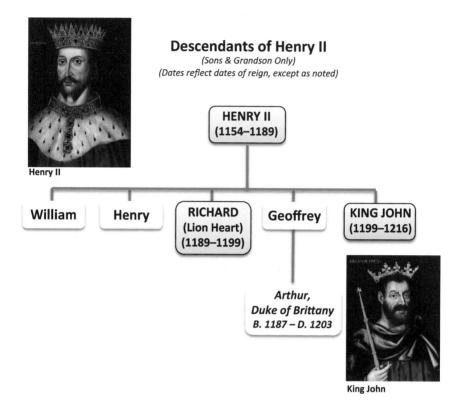

Descendants of Henry II
(Sons & Grandson Only)
(Dates reflect dates of reign, except as noted)

HENRY II
(1154–1189)

Henry II

William   **Henry**   **RICHARD** (Lion Heart) **(1189–1199)**   **Geoffrey**   **KING JOHN** **(1199–1216)**

Arthur,
Duke of Brittany
B. 1187 – D. 1203

King John

Production Note:

In performance King John's speech can generally be delivered to an audience member in the front row, eliminating the need for a second actor to play the role of "Hubert," and any need for Hubert's lines to be recited. (John's deferential responses tell us all we need to know about Hubert's replies.)

This is a technique that can be exploited through much of this play. Direct interactions with the crowd (even shaking hands with the supposed "Hubert," or picking an "Arthur" out of the crowd for "Throw thine eye on yon young boy...") often startle them into joining the world of the play, transporting themselves, imaginatively, into the thirteenth century.

In between these lines,* Hubert replies:

HUBERT: I am much bounden to your majesty. ⟶

* Ellipses (the prolific three dots: "...", used extensively here) never appear in Shakespeare's original. These are provided to cue you, the reader/actor, to an awareness of sequences that have been cut from the portions that are intended for performance. Where there is room (and where the speech was just too delicious to abandon entirely) I will provide the balance of these speeches here, on the left-handed pages. Otherwise, this is all pretty easy to look up.

The life and death of King Iohn.

(1199-1216)
(Span of play's action)

In the thirteenth century, however, issues of succession were not so clear or settled, and while the three-year old Arthur may have had the cleaner path, the thirty-two year old John had all the power. If the name "King John" sounds familiar, he also appears in the many tales of "Robin Hood," as well as "Ivanhoe" and "The Lion In Winter," always depicted as somewhat of a weasel.

For the moment, though, King John was at war with the French, who had taken the side of the now 15-year-old Prince Arthur, who John manages to capture in battle. Knowing the difficulty that Arthur might present to his secure grasp of power, John draws Arthur's captor aside.

KING JOHN
Come hither, Hubert. O my gentle Hubert,
We owe thee much! within this wall of flesh
There is a soul counts thee her creditor
And with advantage means to pay thy love:
And my good friend, thy voluntary oath
Lives in this bosom, dearly cherished.
Give me thy hand. I had a thing to say,
But I will fit it with some better time.
By heaven, Hubert, I am almost ashamed
To say what good respect I have of thee.
…Good friend, thou hast no cause to say so yet,
But thou shalt have; and creep time ne'er so slow,
Yet it shall come from me to do thee good.
I had a thing to say, but let it go:
The sun is in the heaven, and the proud day,
Attended with the pleasures of the world,

7

King John

**KING JOHN
(1199 – 1216)**
(Dates of Reign)

Hubert replies:

HUBERT: So well, that what you bid me undertake,
                   Though that my death were adjunct to my act,
                   By heaven, I would do it.

HUBERT: And I'll keep him so,
                   That he shall not offend your majesty.
                              My Lord?
                                        He shall not live.

Between the original exchange and Hubert's attempted execution of John's implied orders, Hubert is provided with a more explicit, written order to put out Arthur's eyes. This provides Hubert some direct proof of John's guilt (see directly below), so that this argument is not simply a king's word against that of a servant.

HUBERT: Here is your hand and seal for what I did.

KING JOHN *(Continued)*
Is all too wanton and too full of gawds
To give me audience: if the midnight bell
Did, with his iron tongue and brazen mouth,
Sound on into the drowsy race of night;
If this same were a churchyard where we stand,
And thou possessed with a thousand wrongs,
Or if that surly spirit, melancholy,
Had baked thy blood and made it heavy-thick,
Which else runs tickling up and down the veins,
Making that idiot, laughter, keep men's eyes
And strain their cheeks to idle merriment,
A passion hateful to my purposes,
Or if that thou couldst see me without eyes,
Hear me without thine ears, and make reply
Without a tongue, using conceit alone,
Without eyes, ears and harmful sound of words;
Then, in despite of brooded watchful day,
I would into thy bosom pour my thoughts:
But, ah, I will not! yet I love thee well;
And, by my troth, I think thou lovest me well.
…Do not I know thou wouldst?
Good Hubert, Hubert, Hubert, throw thine eye
On yon young boy: I'll tell thee what, my friend,
He is a very serpent in my way;
And whereso'er this foot of mine doth tread,
He lies before me: dost thou understand me?
Thou art his keeper…
Death.
        …A grave.
              …Enough.

Hubert cannot ultimately bring himself to kill the boy, but **pretends** *to have done so, reporting that Arthur is dead. This stirs revolt among the English lords, who jump to the obvious conclusion. John turns on Hubert to blame him for the murder, but when Hubert reminds John that the assassination was, in fact, his idea, John still finds a way to shift the blame.*

KING JOHN
It is the curse of kings to be attended
By slaves that take their humours for a warrant
…How oft the sight of means to do ill deeds

9

HUBERT: My lord—
KING JOHN Hadst thou but shook thy head or made a pause
           When I spake darkly what I purposed,
           Or turn'd an eye of doubt upon my face,
           As bid me tell my tale in express words,
           Deep shame had struck me dumb, made me break off,
           And those thy fears might have wrought fears in me:
           But thou didst understand me by my signs
           And didst in signs again parley with sin;
           Yea, without stop, didst let thy heart consent,
           And consequently thy rude hand to act
           The deed, which both our tongues held vile to name.

The Angevin Empire, After John

In point of fact, King John did not actually sign the Magna Carta, but rather impressed his seal upon it, which was how documents were ratified at the time. This has led to an erroneous legend that John was illiterate, and unable to sign his name. (He did, actually, sign an early draft of the document.)

KING JOHN *(Continued)*
Make deeds ill done! Hadst not thou been by,
A fellow by the hand of nature mark'd,
Quoted and sign'd to do a deed of shame,
This murder had not come into my mind:
But ...Finding thee fit for bloody villany,
Apt, liable to be employ'd in danger,
I faintly broke with thee of Arthur's death;
And thou, to be endeared to a king,
Made it no conscience to destroy a prince.
...Out of my sight, and never see me more!

*Hubert finally reveals that he **hadn't** had the heart to kill the boy, which lends a momentary hope, until it is discovered that Arthur, in the attempt to escape the tower, has fallen to his death... which also looks bad.*

*King John managed to bungle possession of the Angevin Empire, which meant giving most of the English territories in France back to the French. He was ultimately so unpopular and so ineffectual that he was **forced** into doing the thing that is now considered his most significant achievement: signing the Magna Carta in 1215.*

Descendants of King John
(Dates indicate dates of reign)

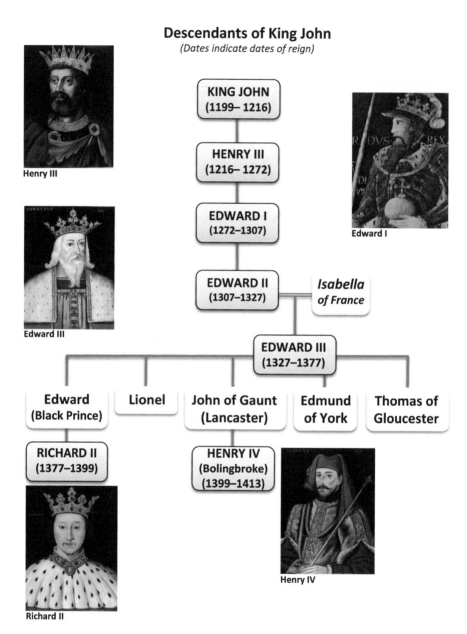

Henry III

Edward III

KING JOHN
(1199– 1216)

HENRY III
(1216– 1272)

EDWARD I
(1272–1307)

Edward I

EDWARD II
(1307–1327)

Isabella of France

EDWARD III
(1327–1377)

Edward
(Black Prince)

Lionel

John of Gaunt
(Lancaster)

Edmund
of York

Thomas of
Gloucester

RICHARD II
(1377–1399)

HENRY IV
(Bolingbroke)
(1399–1413)

Henry IV

Richard II

The first act of **Richard II** finds Richard intervening in a dispute between Henry Bolingbroke and Thomas Mowbray, sentencing both men into exile. When Henry's father, John of Gaunt, dies, Richard takes advantage of Henry's absence to seize Gaunt's estate in order to fund his Irish wars. This move provides Bolingbroke the justification to break his exile and return to England.

The life and death of King Richard the Second.

(1398-1400)
(Span of play)

After King John's death in 1216, a total of only four English Monarchs spanned the 161 years that followed, as Henry III, Edward I, Edward II, and Edward III ruled over a period of relative stability.[5] That last, Edward III, was the product of the marriage between the King of England and the eldest daughter of the King of France.

France freaked out that an English king might **also** rule over **them,** and hauled out the never-before-invoked "Salic Law," which declared that the French monarchy can be passed through the male line only, invalidating Edward's claim through his mother. Defiantly, Edward responds in 1337 by declaring himself King of France, thus beginning the Hundred Years War (which actually continued for 114 years... but who's counting?).

Edward III, like Henry II, a couple of centuries before him, had a bunch of sons, and that generally spells trouble.

Eventually, the crown passed from Edward III to his grandson, Richard, who, being only ten years old at the time, ruled under the supervision of his three uncles, each of whom must have felt at least slightly cheated out of his turn as king.

Decades later, with Richard away in Ireland, struggling and failing to put down an Irish insurrection, his exiled cousin, Henry Bolingbroke, sneaks back into the country, raises an army, assassinates several of Richard's closest companions, and prepares to descend upon the late-returning Richard, himself, who, surrounded by only a small company of soldiers at the time, falls into a despair:

---

[5] "Relative stability:" Edward II had a notoriously troubled reign.

**RICHARD II
(1377–1399)**

Richard II

Richard apparently lingered overlong in Ireland, learning of Bolingbroke's return about a month before he actually came back. There had been an army waiting to support his cause when he returned, but in his long absence, they began to question whether Richard had died in Ireland, and finally gave up their wait and went their several ways. In Shakespeare's telling, they have departed the day before Richard's return.

The abject helplessness of Richard's speech stands in stark contrast to Shakespeare's depiction of another king, also faced with seemingly impossible odds. For a study in the vivid manner in which Shakespeare distinguishes his characters, it is worth examining this speech next to Henry V's "St. Crispin's Day" speech (page 35)... a speech that the often vacillating and defeatist Richard (as Shakespeare paints him) could never have imagined himself giving.

"Sad stories of the death of kings..."

While Richard may well have heard a fair share of "sad stories of the death of kings" over the years, not all of those were stories of "murder." As noted, the four kings immediately preceding Richard all lived out long reigns: Henry III lived to be 65, reigning for 56 of those years. Edward I lived to 68, with a 34-year reign. Only Edward II, who ruled for 20 years, is thought to have been murdered, at the age of 43, probably by the intrigues of his wife, Isabella of France, with her consort, Roger Mortimer. Edward III lived to the age of 64, with 50 of those years spent as king.

Of course, Shakespeare, while writing this play, was probably better acquainted than Richard with legends of murdered English kings, although most of those murders occurred following Richard's death, as the ensuing events will reveal.

KING RICHARD II

No matter where; of comfort no man speak:
Let's talk of graves, of worms, and epitaphs;
Make dust our paper and with rainy eyes
Write sorrow on the bosom of the earth,
Let's choose executors and talk of wills:
And yet not so, for what can we bequeath
Save our deposed bodies to the ground?
Our lands, our lives and all are Bolingbroke's,
And nothing can we call our own but death
And that small model of the barren earth
Which serves as paste and cover to our bones.
For God's sake, let us sit upon the ground
And tell sad stories of the death of kings;
How some have been deposed; some slain in war,
Some haunted by the ghosts they have deposed;
Some poison'd by their wives: some sleeping kill'd;
All murder'd: for within the hollow crown
That rounds the mortal temples of a king
Keeps Death his court and there the antic sits,
Scoffing his state and grinning at his pomp,
Allowing him a breath, a little scene,
To monarchize, be fear'd and kill with looks,
Infusing him with self and vain conceit,
As if this flesh which walls about our life,
Were brass impregnable, and humour'd thus
Comes at the last and with a little pin
Bores through his castle wall, and farewell king!
Cover your heads and mock not flesh and blood
With solemn reverence: throw away respect,
Tradition, form and ceremonious duty,
For you have but mistook me all this while:
I live with bread like you, feel want,
Taste grief, need friends: subjected thus,
How can you say to me, I am a king?

*When Henry Bolingbroke peremptorily attempts to ascend the throne, it sparks a sudden dire prediction from the Bishop of Carlisle. Inevitably, if someone makes a prediction (or, even worse, **a prophecy**!) in a Shakespeare history play, that prophecy comes true... to the letter. (Hindsight being what it is.)*

RICHARD II
(1377–1399)

Richard II

*There are plenty of instances of "English blood" splattering these plays, and perhaps the most immediate manifestations of this "prophecy" are the battles between Henry IV and the rebels which left more than five thousand soldiers dead in its wake, as depicted in **Henry IV, Parts 1 & 2**. But the greater bloodletting comes about several plays later (noted in **Henry VI, Part 3**), as the War of the Roses leaves perhaps forty thousand dead. (Records of the dead at that time were unreliable, and subject to exaggeration, but the Battle of Towton, alone, "the bloodiest battle ever fought on English soil," is said to have left twenty-eight thousand dead.) Given that the issues that led to the War of the Roses can also be traced back to Henry Bolingbroke's sudden takeover, that may be the more likely allusion being made through the foreshadowing of Carlisle's "prophecy."*

And these same thoughts people this little world,
In humours like the people of this world,
For no thought is contented. The better sort,
As thoughts of things divine, are intermix'd
With scruples and do set the word itself
Against the word:
As thus, 'Come, little ones,' and then again,
'It is as hard to come as for a camel
To thread the postern of a small needle's eye.'

And, for they cannot, die in their own pride.

(And none contented:)* sometimes am I king;
Then treasons make me wish myself a beggar,
And so I am: then crushing penury
Persuades me I was better when a king;
Then am I king'd again: and by and by
Think that I am unking'd by Bolingbroke,
And straight am nothing:

* Parentheses indicate a line that's already contained in the passage on the opposite page which is included, here, for continuity.

16

BISHOP OF CARLISLE
If you crown him, let me prophesy:
The blood of English shall manure the ground;
O, if you raise this house against this house,
It will the woefullest division prove
That ever fell upon this cursed earth.
Prevent it, resist it, let it not be so,
Lest child, child's children, cry against you woe!

(Which is what we now have to look forward to…)

Held captive in the tower of London, Richard (sometimes known as the "Poet-King" or the "Actor-King") contemplates:

KING RICHARD II
I have been studying how I may compare
This prison where I live unto the world:
And for because the world is populous
And here is not a creature but myself,
I cannot do it; yet I'll hammer it out.
My brain I'll prove the female to my soul,
My soul the father; and these two beget
A generation of still-breeding thoughts...
Thoughts tending to ambition, they do plot
Unlikely wonders; how these vain weak nails
May tear a passage through the flinty ribs
Of this hard world, my ragged prison walls...
Thoughts tending to content flatter themselves
That they are not the first of fortune's slaves,
Nor shall not be the last; like silly beggars
Who sitting in the stocks refuge their shame,
That many have and others must sit there;
And in this thought they find a kind of ease,
Bearing their own misfortunes on the back
Of such as have before endured the like.
Thus play I in one person many people,
And none contented: …but whate'er I be,
Nor I nor any man that but man is
With nothing shall be pleased, till he be eased
With being nothing.

RICHARD II (1377–1399)

Richard II

HENRY IV (Bolingbroke) (1399–1413)

Henry IV

Shakespeare was evidently intrigued by this back-handedly "innocent" exercise of regal power, and toyed with this conceit several times in his history plays: Already we have seen King John bend over backwards to hint that Hubert must kill Arthur; while Henry asks "Have I no friend will rid me of this living fear?"

But predating both of these entreaties to murder (and probably the inspiration for both) is the famous exhortation by King Henry II, (King John's father), "Will no one rid me of this meddlesome priest?" This very clear hint was taken by four of Henry's knights as a royal command to kill Thomas Becket, the Archbishop of Canterbury. Rather than secure Henry's power, this execution served to make Becket a martyr and a saint.

Shakespeare is quietly asking whether the "Divine Right of Kings" is accompanied by any "divine" moral quality.

*Moments after this speech, Richard is assassinated. Apparently, Henry Bolingbroke (now **King** Henry IV), was overheard muttering, "Have I no friend will rid me of this living fear?" and one of Henry's attendants took this as a directive to murder Richard… Apparently, kings, at the time, had a habit of mentioning their deepest, dearest wishes aloud in the presence of servants and friends who wanted to win their favor.*

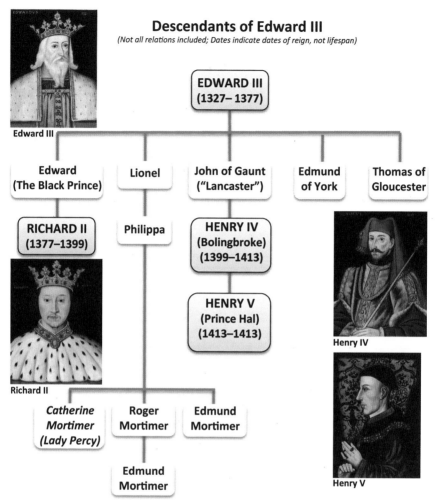

Descendants of Edward III

(Not all relations included; Dates indicate dates of reign, not lifespan)

When Henry Bolingbroke deposes Richard II, he leapfrogs over the rightful claim of the descendants of Lionel, the third son of Edward III. Since the descendants of Lionel claim their right through Philippa, a daughter (and given that Henry has already laid claim to the throne, we assume, without asking), they were given less regard, but with England's criticism of France's selectively-applied "Salic Law," which cheated Edward III out of his French kingship, it would be difficult to argue that this same law should prevail in England. This conflict traces its way through the next several plays, underlying many of these arguments, though rarely mentioned.

Shakespeare, perhaps purposely, conflates the two Edmund Mortimers on this chart, confusing the Edmund Mortimer that is brother-in-law to Henry Percy, and the Edmund Mortimer that is son to Roger Mortimer, who has the direct claim to the English crown. (I make no attempt to clear up this confusion in our performance text, particularly given that it lends greater weight to the plot necessity to keep the elder Edmund in captivity, which is Hotspur's great complaint.)

The First Part of Henry the Fourth

(1402-1403)
(Span of play)

Having stolen the throne from Richard II, Henry IV is dismayed that his eldest son, Prince Hal (also known as Prince Harry or Prince Henry), is keeping an embarrassed distance from the royal court, choosing instead to hang out in taverns with the fat, thieving knight, Sir John Falstaff. As they carouse, the two play-act together, with Falstaff pretending to be Hal's father, the king:

FALSTAFF
Harry... If thou be son to me, why, being son to me, art thou so pointed at? Shall the sun of England prove a thief and take purses? A question to be asked... and yet there is a virtuous man whom I have often noted in thy company, but I know not his name... A goodly portly man, i' faith, and a corpulent; of a cheerful look, a pleasing eye and a most noble carriage; and now I remember me, his name is Falstaff: if that man should be lewdly given, he deceiveth me; for, Harry, I see virtue in his looks. If then the tree may be known by the fruit, as the fruit by the tree, then, there is virtue in that Falstaff: him keep with, the rest banish.

Prince Hal turns the tables on Fallstaff, playing his father in turn, chastising his son for that "old, fat, tun of man... that swollen parcel of dropsies" who follows him about. Falstaff, as Hal, replies...

FALSTAFF
That he is old, the more the pity, his white hairs do witness it; but that he is, saving your reverence, a whoremaster, that I utterly deny. If sack and sugar be a fault, if to be old and merry be a sin, God help the wicked! ...but for sweet Jack Falstaff, true Jack Falstaff, valiant Jack Falstaff, and therefore more valiant, being, as he is, old Jack Falstaff, banish not him thy Harry's company: banish plump Jack, and banish all the world.

Key Family Ties
(Dates indicate dates of reign)

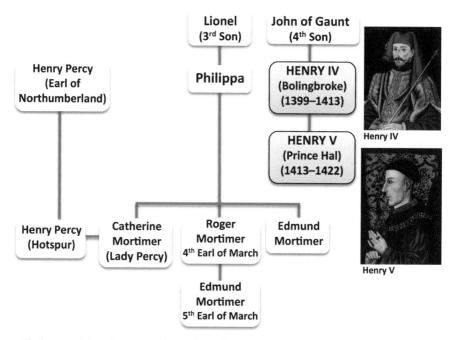

Shakespeare largely invents the notion of Hal and Hotspur being rival sons of rival fathers. The Lord Northumberland (Hotspur's father) was born in 1341, 26 years prior to Henry IV, and his son, Hotspur, was born in 1364, making him three years older than King Henry IV, and twenty-three years older than Prince Hal! In other words, Hotspur would have been more of a "father figure" to Hal.

And yet, a closer "father figure" might have been Richard II, who drew the young Hal into his ranks, even bringing him along on the Irish expedition during his father's exile in France. (This may suggest a personal reason behind Hal's "embarrassed distance" from the court after Richard was deposed.)

"Hotspur's stammer," inspired by Lady Percy's reference to his tendency for "speaking thick," was famously performed by Lawrence Olivier in 1945. Olivier struggled only with the formation of the "w's", a choice which pays off on Hotspur's final line (depicted on page 25).

(And telling me) the sovereign'st thing on earth
Was parmaceti for an inward bruise;
And that it was great pity, so it was,
This villanous salt-petre should be digg'd
Out of the bowels of the harmless earth,
Which many a good tall fellow had destroy'd
So cowardly; and (but for these vile guns...)

22

To which **HAL** *responds:* "I do. I will."

The Percy family, led by Lord Northumberland and his son, Harry Percy, having helped Henry IV depose Richard II, now expects special favors in return, and Harry Percy (better known as "Hotspur" for his hot-headed temperament) wants to trade prisoners he has taken in battles along the Scottish border to ransom home his brother-in-law, Edmund Mortimer. Some suggest that Mortimer has a greater claim to the English crown, which means that Henry wants nothing more than for Mortimer to rot in captivity! Hotspur (sometimes performed with a stammer on a particular consonant) is summoned before King Henry to account for prisoners he has refused to turn over.

HOTSPUR

My liege, I did deny no prisoners.
But I remember, when the fight was done,
When I was dry with rage and extreme toil,
Breathless and faint, leaning upon my sword,
Came there a certain lord, neat, and trimly dress'd,
Fresh as a bridegroom; and his chin new reap'd
Show'd like a stubble-land at harvest-home;
He was perfumed like a milliner;
And 'twixt his finger and his thumb he held
A pouncet-box, which ever and anon
He gave his nose and took't away again;
…and still he smiled and talk'd,
And as the soldiers bore dead bodies by,
He call'd them untaught knaves, unmannerly,
To bring a slovenly unhandsome corse
Betwixt the wind and his nobility.
With many holiday and lady terms
He question'd me; amongst the rest, demanded
My prisoners in your majesty's behalf.
I then, all smarting with my wounds being cold,
To be so pester'd with a popinjay,
Out of my grief and my impatience,
Answer'd neglectingly I know not what,
He should or he should not; for he made me mad
To see him shine so brisk and smell so sweet
And talk so like a waiting-gentlewoman
Of guns and drums and wounds,--God save the mark!--
And telling me [that] but for these vile guns,
He would himself have been a soldier.

Given the great anticipation building up to this scene, it may be of interest to see the actual dressing-down Hal receives from his father (below):

KING HENRY IV

I know not whether God will have it so,
For some displeasing service I have done,
That, in his secret doom, out of my blood
He'll breed revengement and a scourge for me;
But thou dost in thy passages of life
Make me believe that thou art only mark'd
For the hot vengeance and the rod of heaven
To punish my mistreadings. Tell me else,
Could such inordinate and low desires,
Such poor, such bare, such lewd, such mean attempts,
Such barren pleasures, rude society,
As thou art match'd withal and grafted to,
Accompany the greatness of thy blood
And hold their level with thy princely heart?
...Had I so lavish of my presence been,
...So stale and cheap to vulgar company,
Opinion, that did help me to the crown,
Had still kept loyal to possession
And left me in reputeless banishment,
...For thou has lost thy princely privilege
With vile participation: not an eye
But is a-weary of thy common sight...
But wherefore do I tell these news to thee?
Why, Harry, do I tell thee of my foes,
Which art my near'st and dearest enemy?
Thou that art like enough, through vassal fear,
Base inclination and the start of spleen
To fight against me under Percy's pay,
To dog his heels and curtsy at his frowns,
To show how much thou art degenerate.

...this earth that bears thee dead
Bears not alive so stout a gentleman.
If thou wert sensible of courtesy,
I should not make so dear a show of zeal:
But let my favours hide thy mangled face;
And, even in thy behalf, I'll thank myself
For doing these fair rites of tenderness.
(Adieu, and take thy praise with thee to heaven!)*
Thy ignominy sleep with thee in the grave,
But not remember'd in thy epitaph!

HOTSPUR *(Continued)*
This bald unjointed chat of his, my lord,
I answer'd indirectly, as I said;
And I beseech you, let not his report
Come current for an accusation
Betwixt my love and your high majesty.

The dispute between the Percys and King Henry escalates into an all-out war, and Prince Hal, chastised (as predicted) by his father for his loose ways, and guilt-tripped for Northumberland's son being the better soldier, swears his resolve to "redeem all this on Percy's head."

And the thing that pretty much never happens in real life, miraculously comes about in this instance (as it does in most of these plays) as, amid the melee of a chaotic battle, with thousands of soldiers on either side, Hotspur and Hal face off in single man-to-man combat, even as Falstaff runs away and pretends to be dead. Hal defeats Hotspur, who dies in Hal's arms,[6] lamenting...

HOTSPUR
O, Harry, thou hast robb'd me of my youth!
I better brook the loss of brittle life
Than those proud titles thou hast won of me;
...But thought's the slave of life, and life time's fool;
                    ...O, I could prophesy,
But that the earthy and cold hand of death
Lies on my tongue: no, Percy, thou art dust
And food for—

PRINCE HENRY
For worms, brave Percy: fare thee well, great heart!
Ill-weaved ambition, how much art thou shrunk!
When that this body did contain a spirit,
A kingdom for it was too small a bound;
But now two paces of the vilest earth
Is room enough:
...Adieu, and take thy praise with thee to heaven!

---

[6] For the record, Shakespeare never indicates that Hotspur "dies in Hal's arms..." but it makes a fun moment (when performed as a one-person show), when Hotspur's line, delivered from below (as if he is being held), transitions to Hal's response, as the actor shifts to pantomime a position of holding the now-lifeless body from above.

*While Falstaff no longer furthers the story of Hal's eventual succession, he remained a popular character in **Henry IV, Part 2**, which, Asimov suggests may have been written to satisfy demands for more of this wildly popular character.*

*And yet, this second **Henry IV** play does return us to the theme of succession in full force with the anticipated death of King Henry, at the same time as it touches on another favorite theme of Shakespeare's: That regardless of how powerful a character may be, even the king, himself, suffers from all of the same human frailties that the rest of us face:*

KING HENRY IV

How many thousand of my poorest subjects
Are at this hour asleep! O sleep, O gentle sleep,
Nature's soft nurse, how have I frighted thee,
That thou no more wilt weigh my eyelids down
And steep my senses in forgetfulness?...
O thou dull god, why liest thou with the vile
In loathsome beds, and leavest the kingly couch
A watch-case or a common 'larum-bell?
Wilt thou upon the high and giddy mast
Seal up the ship-boy's eyes, and rock his brains
In cradle of the rude imperious surge...?
Canst thou, O partial sleep, give thy repose
To the wet sea-boy in an hour so rude,
And in the calmest and most stillest night,
With all appliances and means to boot,
Deny it to a king? Then happy low, lie down!
Uneasy lies the head that wears a crown.

HENRY IV
(Bolingbroke)
(1399–1413)

Henry IV

Let all the tears that should bedew my hearse
Be drops of balm to sanctify thy head:

Pluck down my officers, break my decrees;
For now a time is come to mock at form:
Harry the Fifth is crown'd: up, vanity!
Down, royal state! all you sage counsellors, hence!

The Second Part of Henry the Fourth, Containing his Death : and the Coronation of King Henry the Fift.

(1403-1413)
(Span of play)

    King Henry IV falls into a steep decline, marked particularly by the insomnia from which he suffers, leading him to ruminate, famously, "Uneasy lies the head that wears the crown." When he finally falls into a deep sleep, Prince Hal mistakenly assumes that his father has died, and, lifting the crown from the pillow next to him, goes off to contemplate the heavy burden he now faces. When he awakens, King Henry confronts his son:

KING HENRY IV
Thou hast stolen that which after some few hours
Were thine without offence; and at my death
Thou hast seal'd up my expectation:
Thy life did manifest thou lovedst me not,
And thou wilt have me die assured of it.
Thou hidest a thousand daggers in thy thoughts,
Which thou hast whetted on thy stony heart,
To stab at half an hour of my life.
What! canst thou not forbear me half an hour?
Then get thee gone and dig my grave thyself,
And bid the merry bells ring to thine ear
That thou art crowned, not that I am dead.
…Only compound me with forgotten dust
Give that which gave thee life unto the worms.
…Now, neighbour confines, purge you of your scum:
Have you a ruffian that will swear, drink, dance,
Revel the night, rob, murder, and commit
The oldest sins the newest kind of ways?
Be happy, he will trouble you no more;

As this scene touches the very deliberate passing of the crown from one king to the next, it is probably worth a longer look (below):

PRINCE HENRY

O, pardon me, my liege! ...There is your crown;
And He that wears the crown immortally
Long guard it yours! ...
God witness with me, when I here came in,
And found no course of breath within your majesty,
How cold it struck my heart! ...
Coming to look on you, thinking you dead,
And dead almost, my liege, to think you were,
I spake unto this crown as having sense,
And thus upbraided it: 'The care on thee depending
Hath fed upon the body of my father;
Therefore, thou best of gold art worst of gold:'
...Accusing it, I put it on my head,
To try with it, as with an enemy
That had before my face murder'd my father,
But if it did infect my blood with joy,
Or swell my thoughts to any strain of pride...
Let God for ever keep it from my head!

KING HENRY IV

O my son,
God put it in thy mind to take it hence,
That thou mightst win the more thy father's love,
Pleading so wisely in excuse of it!
...God knows, my son,
By what by-paths and indirect crook'd ways
I met this crown; and I myself know well
How troublesome it sat upon my head.
To thee it shall descend with better quiet,
Better opinion, better confirmation;
For all the soil of the achievement goes
With me into the earth ...for what in me was purchased,
Falls upon thee in a more fairer sort....
(How I came by the crown, O God forgive;
And grant it may with thee in true peace live!)

PRINCE HENRY

My gracious liege,
You won it, wore it, kept it, gave it me;
Then plain and right must my possession be:
Which I with more than with a common pain
'Gainst all the world will rightfully maintain.

Henry V

28

England shall double gild his treble guilt,
England shall give him office, honour, might;
For the fifth Harry from curb'd licence plucks
The muzzle of restraint, and the wild dog
Shall flesh his tooth on every innocent.
O my poor kingdom, sick with civil blows!
When that my care could not withhold thy riots,
What wilt thou do when riot is thy care?
O, thou wilt be a wilderness again,
Peopled with wolves, thy old inhabitants!

Once again, Hal manages to quell his father's doubts in moving terms and, reconciled with his son, King Henry dies, pleading:

KING HENRY IV
How I came by the crown, O, God forgive,
And grant it may with thee in true peace live.

    Prince Hal, now "King Henry V," surprises everyone by banishing Falstaff from his presence, thus shaking off any taint of corruption that might attach itself to the crown.

Henry V

CHORUS

     But pardon, and gentles all,
The flat unraised spirits that have dared
On this unworthy scaffold to bring forth
So great an object: can this cockpit hold
The vasty fields of France? or may we cram
Within this wooden O the very casques
That did affright the air at Agincourt?
...Let us, ciphers to this great accompt,
On your imaginary forces work...
Piece out our imperfections with your thoughts;
Into a thousand parts divide one man,
And make imaginary puissance;
Think when we talk of horses, that you see them
Printing their proud hoofs i' the receiving earth;
For 'tis your thoughts that now must deck our kings,
Carry them here and there; jumping o'er times,
Turning the accomplishment of many years
Into an hour-glass: for the which supply,
Admit me Chorus to this history;
Who prologue-like your humble patience pray,
Gently to hear, kindly to judge, our play.

  Shakespeare goes to great lengths to detail the French "Salique Law," and the Archbishop of Canterbury pooh-poohs it in justifying Henry's claim:

ARCHBISHOP OF CANTERBURY

There is no bar
To make against your highness' claim to France
But this, which they produce from Pharamond:
'No woman shall succeed in Salique land.'
...Where Charles the Great, having subdued the Saxons,
There left behind and settled certain French;
Who, holding in disdain the German women
For some dishonest manners of their life,
Establish'd then this law...

    ...we understand him well,
How he comes o'er us with our wilder days,
Not measuring what use we made of them.
... But tell the Dauphin I will keep my state,
Be like a king and show my sail of greatness
When I do rouse me in my throne of France:
For that I have laid by my majesty
And plodded like a man for working-days,
But I will rise there with so full a glory
That I will dazzle all the eyes of France,
Yea, strike the Dauphin blind to look on us.

The Life of Henry the Fift.

(1414-1420)
(Span of play)

With Henry V, Shakespeare finally has a character of heroic proportions to *celebrate*:

Chorus
O for a Muse of fire, that would ascend
The brightest heaven of invention,
A kingdom for a stage, princes to act
And monarchs to behold the swelling scene!
Then should the warlike Harry, like himself,
Assume the port of Mars; and at his heels,
Leash'd in like hounds, should famine, sword and fire
Crouch for employment...

King Henry decides that it is finally time to press for his ancient right to the French crown, and the French Prince, the "Dauphin" responds by sending an ambassador with the gift of a box of tennis balls: a mockery of the king's reckless and irresponsible youth.

KING HENRY V
We are glad the Dauphin is so pleasant with us;
When we have match'd our rackets to these balls,
We will, in France, by God's grace, play a set
Shall strike his father's crown into the hazard.
...And tell the pleasant prince this mock of his
Hath turn'd his balls to gun-stones;...
For many a thousand widows
Shall this his mock mock out of their dear husbands;
Mock mothers from their sons, mock castles down;

Disguise fair nature with hard-favour'd rage;
Then lend the eye a terrible aspect;
Let pry through the portage of the head
Like the brass cannon; let the brow o'erwhelm it
As fearfully as doth a galled rock
O'erhang and jutty his confounded base,
Swill'd with the wild and wasteful ocean.

    ...On, on, you noblest English.
Whose blood is fet from fathers of war-proof!
Fathers that, like so many Alexanders,
Have in these parts from morn till even fought
And sheathed their swords for lack of argument:
Dishonour not your mothers; now attest
That those whom you call'd fathers did beget you.
Be copy now to men of grosser blood,
And teach them how to war. And you, good yeoman,
Whose limbs were made in England, show us here
The mettle of your pasture; let us swear
That you are worth your breeding; which I doubt not;
For there is none of you so mean and base,
That hath not noble lustre in your eyes.
I see you stand like greyhounds in the slips,
Straining upon the start.

While Henry was ultimately to prevail at Harfleur, it was a long five-week siege, with sickness, death and desertion diminishing Henry's forces, and winter coming on. Between losses in the fighting, and the need to leave troops behind to hold Harfleur against any retaliating French siege, Henry left Harfleur with only about a third of the men that he had arrived with. This made any continued aggressive march toward Paris impossible, leading Henry into a "side-step" toward Calais, which was already a secure English strong-hold.

The "Dauphin scene" is our biggest "cheat" in this adaptation. It is a series of one-liners extracted from two **different** characters. We discover the Dauphin, and the Duke of Orleans twitting each other over who has the better armor, the better horse, and the best mistress (jokingly confusing their horses with their mistresses). While the Dauphin has the opening lines, most of the subsequent speeches (assigned here to the Dauphin) are spoken by the Duke of Orleans (who, for the record, seems to be an even more supercilious twit than the Dauphin).

KING HENRY V *(Continued)*
And some are yet ungotten and unborn
That shall have cause to curse the Dauphin's scorn.

Henry begins his campaign in France, laying siege to the castle at Harfleur, driving his men on.

KING HENRY V
Once more unto the breach, dear friends, once more;
Or close the wall up with our English dead.
In peace there's nothing so becomes a man
As modest stillness and humility:
But when the blast of war blows in our ears,
Then imitate the action of the tiger;
Stiffen the sinews, summon up the blood…
Now set the teeth and stretch the nostril wide,
Hold hard the breath and bend up every spirit
To his full height. …The game's afoot:
Follow your spirit, and upon this charge
Cry "God for Harry, England, and Saint George!"

King Henry eventually prevails at Harfleur, and, leaving a garrison behind, turns eastward toward Calais with a much smaller army, but finds himself cut off by the vast French army (outnumbering them by perhaps 5-to-1) at Agincourt. The night before their decisive battle, the French Dauphin scoffs over the pitiful English forces, wishing that the morning, and its ensuing battle, would come that much the sooner. (Keep in mind that this is an English playwright's depiction of the hated French):

DAUPHIN
I will trot to-morrow a mile, and my way shall be paved with English faces… What a wretched and peevish fellow is this king of England, to mope with his fat-brained followers so far out of his knowledge!…
That's a valiant flea that dare eat his breakfast on the lip of a lion.
… It is now two o'clock: but, let me see, by ten
We shall have each a hundred Englishmen.

Meanwhile, on the other side of the divide, Henry moves amongst his men, encouraging them, finding some wishing for reinforcements from those left behind, now sleeping comfortably in England.

What's he that wishes so?
My cousin Westmoreland? No, my fair cousin:
If we are mark'd to die, we are enough
To do our country loss; and if to live,
The fewer men, the greater share of honour.
God's will! I pray thee, wish not one man more.

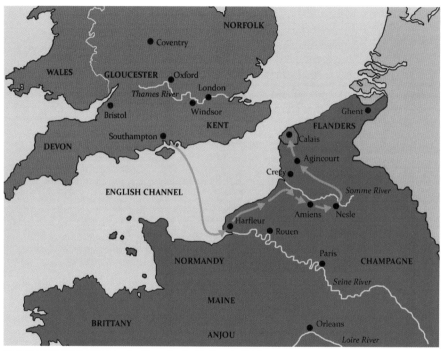

Henry's interrupted path from Southampton to Harfleur to Calais

Henry's march to Calais with an army of fifteen-thousand, made good time at first, reaching the Somme River in only five days, but found themselves forced into a long, excruciating run-around by French troops blocking the river's crossing which was to prove devastating to their troop strength. They were repeatedly stymied in their efforts to find a position where they might ford the river without coming under French fire. Surviving on the barest of provisions, a starving, bedraggled company of twelve-thousand arrived in Agincourt some sixteen days after setting out from Harfleur, facing an estimated "full three-score thousand" (60,000) French.

KING HENRY V

...By Jove, I am not covetous for gold,
Nor care I who doth feed upon my cost;
It yearns me not if men my garments wear;
Such outward things dwell not in my desires:
But if it be a sin to covet honour,
I am the most offending soul alive.
No, faith, my coz, wish not a man from England:
God's peace! I would not lose so great an honour
As one man more, methinks, would share from me
For the best hope I have. O, do not wish one more!
Rather proclaim it, Westmoreland, through my host,
That he which hath no stomach to this fight,
Let him depart; his passport shall be made
And crowns for convoy put into his purse:
We would not die in that man's company
That fears his fellowship to die with us.
This day is called the feast of Crispian:
He that outlives this day, and comes safe home,
Will stand a tip-toe when the day is named,
And rouse him at the name of Crispian.
He that shall live this day, and see old age,
Will yearly on the vigil feast his neighbours,
And say 'To-morrow is Saint Crispian:'
Then will he strip his sleeve and show his scars.
And say 'These wounds I had on Crispin's day.'
Old men forget: yet all shall be forgot,
But he'll remember with advantages
What feats he did that day: then shall our names.
Familiar in his mouth as household words
Harry the king, Bedford and Exeter,
Warwick and Talbot, Salisbury and Gloucester,
Be in their flowing cups freshly remember'd.
This story shall the good man teach his son;
And Crispin Crispian shall ne'er go by,
From this day to the ending of the world,
But we in it shall be remember'd;
We few, we happy few, we band of brothers;
For he to-day that sheds his blood with me
Shall be my brother; be he ne'er so vile,
This day shall gentle his condition:
And gentlemen in England now a-bed

As the sequence is presented in the play, we might be tempted to assume that Henry moves directly from his conquest at Agincourt (which was in 1415) to the signing of the peace treaty. This is not at all the case: Henry returned to England, his navy fought off a challenge to the English garrison at Harfleur, and fought yet another campaign, even more decisive than Agincourt, from 1417 to 1419, which culminated in the French surrender at Paris.

Shakespeare never addresses the madness of King Charles, despite the fact that most of his audience would be well aware of it. This is likely because this madness which appears in King Charles, as well as his grandson, Henry VI, may be suggested to live in the bloodline that has produced Queen Elizabeth, Shakespeare's own monarch. And for Shakespeare to draw attention to this would clearly cross the lines of decorum lay.

There ensues, in the midst of this dialogue with Kate, a rather extended back-and-forth, in which Henry tells most of the good jokes, and Kate fails to understand what he means...

KING HENRY V

Now, fie upon my false French! By mine honour, in true English, I love thee, Kate: by which honour I dare not swear thou lovest me; yet my blood begins to flatter me that thou dost, notwithstanding the poor and untempering effect of my visage. Now, beshrew my father's ambition! he was thinking of civil wars when he got me: therefore was I created with a stubborn outside, with an aspect of iron, that, when I come to woo ladies, I fright them. But, in faith, Kate, the elder I wax, the better I shall appear: my comfort is, that old age, that ill layer up of beauty, can do no more spoil upon my face: thou hast me, if thou hast me, at the worst; and thou shalt wear me, if thou wear me, better and better: (and therefore) tell me, most fair Katharine, will you have me? (Put off your maiden blushes;) avouch the thoughts of your heart with the looks of an empress; (take me by the hand...)

"Mostly heroic" alludes to what is sometimes described as King Henry's war crimes: the killing of women, children, and prisoners. Shakespeare justifies some of this as a retaliation against ruthless French prisoners who have killed young boys who were left to guard the baggage, but even Shakespeare peels back the heroism to reveal the ruthless horrors of this war, as, earlier in the play, amid the siege of Harfleur, he depicted Henry threatening the civilian population:

KING HENRY V

If not, why, in a moment look to see
The blind and bloody soldier with foul hand
Defile the locks of your shrill-shrieking daughters;
Your fathers taken by the silver beards,
And their most reverend heads dash'd to the walls,
Your naked infants spitted upon pikes,
Whiles the mad mothers with their howls confused
Do break the clouds...

KING HENRY V *(Continued)*
Shall think themselves accursed they were not here,
And hold their manhoods cheap whiles any speaks
That fought with us upon Saint Crispin's day.

King Henry wins an astonishing victory at Agincourt, and the French terms of surrender include the French Princess Katharine as bride in the deal. Henry and Katharine (also known as "Kate") are left behind to work out romantic terms to their relationship, while Henry's lieutenants go off to discuss political terms with the French King (sometimes quietly known as "King Charles the Mad"). Kate, who barely speaks any English, asks...

KATHARINE
Is it possible dat I sould love de enemy of France?

KING HENRY V
No, it is not possible you should love the enemy of France, Kate, but in loving me you should love the friend of France, for I love France so well that I will not part with a village of it; I will have it all mine: and, Kate, when France is mine and I am yours, then yours is France and you are mine... and therefore, put off your maiden blushes; take me by the hand, and say 'Harry of England I am thine:' which word thou shalt no sooner bless mine ear withal, but I will tell thee aloud 'England is thine, Ireland is thine, France is thine, and Harry Plantagenet is thine.'

For one brief shining moment, all looks bright for England, as their (mostly) heroic King flexes English muscle in England, Ireland and France. Henry and Kate are married in 1420; their son, another Henry, is born in 1421. And with the anticipated death of King Charles the Mad (who died in 1422), a king of England will finally sit atop the thrones of both England and France!

*At least he **would** have, had Henry not died two months **before** King Charles the Mad, at the very young age of 35, of dysentery, leaving behind an eight-month old infant king to hold it all together.*

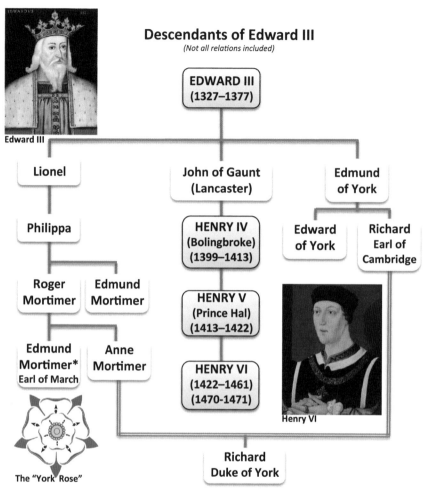

Descendants of Edward III
(Not all relations included)

EDWARD III
(1327–1377)

Lionel

John of Gaunt
(Lancaster)

Edmund
of York

Philippa

HENRY IV
(Bolingbroke)
(1399–1413)

Edward
of York

Richard
Earl of
Cambridge

Roger
Mortimer

Edmund
Mortimer

HENRY V
(Prince Hal)
(1413–1422)

Edmund
Mortimer*
Earl of March

Anne
Mortimer

HENRY VI
(1422–1461)
(1470-1471)

Henry VI

The "York Rose"

Richard
Duke of York

Richard of York is twice descended from Edward III, through both Edward's third son, Lionel, and Edward's fifth son, Edmund. His royal claim is via Lionel, but that line passes through two female heirs (Philippa and Anne) along the way. He is called Richard Plantagenet through much of Shakespeare's play. We avoid the confusion of yet another name to remember, referring to him only as the "Duke of York," a title that is not actually awarded him until Act III of this play.

Shakespeare's play never mentions the particular legal argument that leads these English lords to choose sides, plucking white roses vs. red roses. Clearly, they cannot argue directly over their own right to the crown, as that would be treason. But they might disguise the advocacy of their own royal merit behind a more abstract argument over the "Salic Law" which was such an important focus of Henry V's claim to France. York might, with some justification, take the anti-Salic side (secretly expecting to claim the crown through a female line of the family tree). Somerset would naturally oppose this, given that (though tainted with illegitimacy) he can, at least, claim an unbroken male line of decent.

The firſt Part of Henry the Sixt.

(1422-1445)

It was a feeding frenzy.

Immediately, young Henry's uncles form a "Regency Council," and proceed to fight amongst themselves for control over the child king and management of the French wars.

*Those who were not working to rule **through** young Henry, were looking to set themselves up as the **next** king.*

*The Duke of York learns from his dying uncle, Edmund Mortimer (the same Mortimer that Henry IV wanted to see rot in captivity)[7], that his descent from Lionel, the third son of Edward III, makes him a better choice than Henry, who is descended by way of Edward III's **fourth** son, John of Gaunt.*

*This drives a wedge between York and Somerset, who is the son of one of John of Gaunt's bastard sons (who was "legitimized" when the prolific Gaunt married his mistress as his third wife). Somerset **also** sees himself as next in line to the throne, given that the child King Henry has, of course, as of yet, no heirs.*

*The challenge to York is to get enough people to **notice** that he has the better credentials, without getting charged with treason and having his head chopped off in the process. He adopts the symbol of the white rose, whereby his sympathizers can quietly signify their support, wearing it in their lapel... or, wherever.*

---

[7] See page 20: This streamlined adaptation continues Shakespeare's conflation of the two Edmund Mortimers. For the record, the elder Edmund (Hotspur's Brother-in-Law), who died in 1409, was never a rival successor to the Lancaster (Henry's) line. The younger Edmund (the more direct heir) died in 1425, and it would have been him that York (who was still "Richard Plantagenet" at the time), met with for this deathbed conversation.

Descendants of John of Gaunt: The House of Lancaster
(Not all relations included)

```
Blanche ——— John of Gaunt ——— Catherine
             Duke of Lancaster
```

Mary de Bohun — **HENRY IV** (Bolingbroke) (1399–1413)

John Beaufort Earl of Somerset | Henry Beaufort Bishop of Winchester | Thomas Beaufort Duke of Exeter

Katherine of France — **HENRY V** (Prince Hal) (1413–1422)

Humphrey Duke of Gloucester

John Duke of Somerset

Edmund Duke of Somerset

HENRY VI (1422–1461) (1470-1471)

The "Lancaster Rose"

Henry VI

Where is my other life? mine own is gone;
O, where's young Talbot? where is valiant John?

When he perceived me shrink and on my knee,
His bloody sword he brandish'd over me,
And, like a hungry lion, did commence
Rough deeds of rage and stern impatience;
But when my angry guardant stood alone,
Tendering my ruin and assail'd of none,
Dizzy-eyed fury and great rage of heart
Suddenly made him from my side to start
Into the clustering battle of the French;
(And in that sea of blood my boy) did drench
His over-mounting spirit, and (there died,
My Icarus, my blossom, in his pride.)

John of Gaunt was never King, but he had a knack for marrying well and, perhaps, teaching his children that same talent. He became Duke of Lancaster shortly after marrying Lancaster's daughter. Their daughter became Queen of Portugal by marriage, and their son, who also married an heiress, became King Henry IV. Gaunt's second wife was daughter to the King of Castile, but Gaunt failed to claim that crown (though a daughter from this marriage became Queen of Castile, also by marriage). Between wives and mistresses, there were at least sixteen children of John's issue.

The Order of the Garter (established by King Edward III) to which Talbot belongs, demands strict adherence to principles of honor, honesty, valor and loyalty, which are violated by both York and Suffolk, who are driven by narcissism and personal gain. Shakespeare, likewise, depicts a scene in which Talbot strips a "Sir John Fastolfe" (probably a model for Jack Falstaff of **Henry IV**) of his garter, accusing him of deserting the battlefield.

40

YORK (Richard Plantagenet)

Since you are tongue-tied and so loath to speak,
In dumb significants proclaim your thoughts:
Let him that is a true-born gentleman,
If he suppose that I have pleaded truth,
From off this brier pluck a white rose with me.

*Eventually, the followers of Somerset choose the **Red Rose** as their calling card, and the War of the Roses (a simultaneous, **intramural**, war between English lords) is on! In the course of their petty squabbles, both York and Somerset evade coming to the assistance of an actual English war hero, Sir John Talbot, each preferring to exploit the other's failure as an opportunity for blame. Unfortunately, it is just at this moment that Talbot's son, "Young Talbot," arrives to join his father's forces for his first actual taste of battle. Unwilling to stain the family name by running away, young Talbot dies in battle, as his father, also dying, laments:*

TALBOT

...Triumphant death, smear'd with captivity,
Young Talbot's valour makes me smile at thee:
...[For] in that sea of blood my boy... there died,
My Icarus, my blossom, in his pride.
...Poor boy! he smiles, methinks, as who should say,
Had death been French, then death had died to-day.

Joan of Arc is France's most celebrated Military hero, and was, in fact, canonized as a saint in 1920... a little late to save her from burning at the stake in 1431.

*But to the English, who grew up on tales of English soldiers beating up on French armies, even when outnumbered 5-to-1, being beaten **by** the French was impossible, especially when those French were being led by **a woman!***

*To them there could be only one possible explanation: Joan of Arc was not a Saint, but a **witch!***

**Joan of Arc
(Joan la Pucelle)**

The narcissism and cowardice of York, Suffolk and Fastolfe are surpassed only by the ill deeds of the French, who, reliant on a "witch" to win victories in battle, have performed an even greater affront to the code of chivalry. Shakespeare (or Shakespeare's co-author) clearly join in the English prejudice against Joan.

Joan of Arc, originally named, Jeanne Darc (shortned to Jeanne D'Arc, which lead to the misnomer Joan of Arc), is known as Joan la Pucelle (Joan the Maid) in Shakespeare's play. This is intended to denote (or perhaps to mock) Joan's professed virginity, a state called into question later in the play, when Joan claims to be with child in order to avoid being burned at the stake. (Joan's reputation, further darkened by this play, was not rehabilitated until well after the Elizabethan era.)

(See, they forsake me!) Now the time is come
That France must vail her lofty-plumed crest
And let her head fall into England's lap.
(My ancient incantations are too weak,
And hell too strong for me to buckle with:
Now, France, thy glory droopeth to the dust.)
                                        Exit
Excursions. Re-enter JOAN LA PUCELLE fighting hand to hand with YORK. JOAN LA PUCELLE is taken. The French fly.

Henry VI, Part 1 *makes little attempt to follow actual history, especially when compared to Shakespeare's other plays. It has been conjectured that this play is either a "doctored up" version of another playwright's work, or a collaborative venture from the early days of Shakespeare's career. There is some evidence that Parts 2 and 3 were originally considered Parts 1 and 2 of Shakespeare's series, which suggests that this earlier play was reworked by Shakespeare to function as a "prequel."*

While the Elizabethan audience would clearly want to blame Margaret for all of the ills of Henry's monarchy, beginning with the botched "dowry" (see page 45), it is more likely that the loss of these French territories was already near complete, and the "dowry" was simply an acknowledgement of the situation as it already stood on the ground. It secured Anjou for England as a strategic partner against other French territories, strengthening the grip over those few English territories that remained.

This marriage arrangement was settled in 1445, also preceding the death of Talbot. This play jumps forward and backward in time, most likely to pluck out events that would satisfy the Elizabethan audience's nationalistic preferences.

JOAN LA PUCELLE

(Thunder, Enter Fiends)

Now, ye familiar spirits, that are cull'd
Out of the powerful regions under earth,
Help me this once, that France may get the field.

(They walk, and speak not)

O, hold me not with silence over-long!
Where I was wont to feed you with my blood,
I'll lop a member off and give it you,
So you do condescend to help me now.

(They hang their heads)

No hope to have redress? My body shall
Pay recompense, if you will grant my suit.

(They shake their heads)

Cannot my body nor blood-sacrifice
Entreat you to your wonted furtherance?
Then take my soul, my body, soul and all,
Before that England give the French the foil.

(They depart)

See, they forsake me!...
My ancient incantations are too weak,
And hell too strong for me to buckle with:
Now, France, thy glory droopeth to the dust.

*Shakespeare depicts this failure of Joan (who, we remember, died in 1431) at least 22 years later, **after** the death of Talbot, who died in 1453. Seemingly, Shakespeare (or his co-author in this very early play of his career) had an interest in emphasizing English victories, even as the collapse of the English grasp of French territories was well underway and perhaps irreversible.*

Henry VI, Part 1 concludes with yet another English victory, this time over Anjou: the Duke of Suffolk captures Margaret, the fifteen-year-old daughter of the Duke of Anjou, an act that must have sent a shudder through the collective spine of the Elizabethan audience who surely know what is coming.

Suffolk falls in love with Margaret, but, given that he is already married, decides to pimp her out to King Henry instead.

In this instance, it is clear that Henry is a pawn in Suffolk's hands (though he was also beholden to Margaret, Gloucester, and just about anyone who was forceful enough). Suffolk has dizzied the king with tales of Margaret's beauty, and was widely blamed for the terms of this "dowry" (which finds the payment coming from the husband's side, and not the wife's). While that dowry was widely viewed as a betrayal, these territories were already slipping from English grasp, and the marriage agreement simply gave the public someone to blame.

A major justification for Margaret's "dowry" was that her father, the Duke of Anjou, was also the "King of Naples", yet this was a title held more in theory than practice.

I cannot blame them all: what is't to them?
'Tis thine they give away, and not their own.
Pirates may make cheap pennyworths of their pillage
And purchase friends and give to courtezans,
Still revelling like lords till all be gone;
While as the silly owner of the goods
Weeps over them and wrings his hapless hands
And shakes his head and trembling stands aloof,
While all is shared and all is borne away,
Ready to starve and dare not touch his own:
So York must sit and fret and bite his tongue,
While his own lands are bargain'd for and sold.
Methinks the realms of England, France and Ireland
Bear that proportion to my flesh and blood
As did the fatal brand Althaea burn'd
Unto the prince's heart of Calydon.
Anjou and Maine both given unto the French!
Cold news for me, for I had hope of France,
Even as I have of fertile England's soil.
A day will come when York shall claim his own;
And therefore I will take the Nevils' parts
And make a show of love to proud Duke Humphrey,
And, when I spy advantage, claim the crown,
For that's the golden mark I seek to hit:
Nor shall proud Lancaster usurp my right,
Nor hold the sceptre in his childish fist,
Nor wear the diadem upon his head,
Whose church-like humours fits not for a crown.

Henry had been crowned King of England in 1431, fourteen years before his 1445 marriage, and was also crowned the (contested) King of France in 1431. As such, Henry (the heir of the house of Lancaster) has certainly "held the scepter in his childish fist," and "worn the diadem upon his head" by now... though perhaps York (above) is speaking figuratively, acknowledging that the king has yet to seize any significant power.

The second Part of Henry the Sixt,

(1445-1455)

Henry, now 24 years old, but still very much a pawn, gives up hard-won territories in France for Margaret's hand in marriage, which is not how "dowries" are supposed to work.

This creates a quiet uproar among the English lords, none less than York, who increasingly sees himself as rightful heir to the throne.

YORK
Anjou and Maine are given to the French;
Paris is lost; the state of Normandy
Stands on a tickle point, now they are gone:
Suffolk concluded on the articles,
The peers agreed, and Henry was well pleased
To change two dukedoms for a duke's fair daughter.
…Then, York, be still awhile, till time do serve:
Watch thou and wake when others be asleep,
To pry into the secrets of the state;
Till Henry, surfeiting in joys of love,
With his new bride and England's dear-bought queen,
And Humphrey, with the peers, be fall'n at jars;
Then will I raise aloft the milk-white rose,
With whose sweet smell the air shall be perfumed;
And in my standard bear the arms of York
To grapple with the house of Lancaster;
And, force perforce, I'll make him yield the crown,
Whose bookish rule hath pull'd fair England down.

Gloucester's enemies struggled to get him to step down from his role of "Lord Protector," a role that the king seemed happy to let him continue in long after he was of age to rule. When the other lords argued that the king was now of an age to make his own decisions, it would have been difficult and indelicate for Gloucester to point out that, in spite of his age, Henry remained a child for most of his life.

The slandering of Gloucester largely took the form of an attack against his second wife, Eleanor Cobham, who was discovered indulging in witchcraft to advance her husband's interests.

King Henry does not instantly jump to the conclusion of Suffolk's guilt, but a popular uprising reveals that the public (among whom Gloucester was a powerful figure of chivalry) had come to that conclusion, and demanded Suffolk's punishment. [In reality, Suffolk's exile had nothing do to with Gloucester's murder.] In Shakespeare's play, much of Henry's convincing is achieved by the Earl of Warwick in a speech which is an amusing forerunner of forensic detective drama:

WARWICK
See how the blood is settled in his face.
Oft have I seen a timely-parted ghost,
Of ashy semblance, meagre, pale and bloodless,
Being all descended to the labouring heart;
Who, in the conflict that it holds with death,
Attracts the same for aidance 'gainst the enemy;
Which with the heart there cools and ne'er returneth
To blush and beautify the cheek again.
But see, his face is black and full of blood,
His eye-balls further out than when he lived,
Staring full ghastly like a strangled man;
His hair uprear'd, his nostrils stretched with struggling;
His hands abroad display'd, as one that grasp'd
And tugg'd for life and was by strength subdued:
Look, on the sheets his hair you see, is sticking;
His well-proportion'd beard made rough and rugged,
Like to the summer's corn by tempest lodged.
It cannot be but he was murder'd here;
The least of all these signs were probable.

> Thou hast appointed justices of peace, to call poor men
> before them about matters they were not able to answer.
> Moreover, thou hast put them in prison; and because they
> could not read, thou hast hanged them; when, indeed,
> only for that cause they have been most worthy to live.

Cade's anti-authoritarian, anti-intellectual stance seems defiantly ignorant, but there was at least one bit of justification. There was a "benefit of clergy" clause in the law, which exempted anyone who could read a passage of the Bible (which at this time was mostly members of the clergy) from execution, which left the average, illiterate man, subject to more severe punishment, seemingly for their inability to read. Cade is reversing that injustice.

The English Lords jockey for power and position, and decide that what they really need is to get rid of Humphrey, the Duke of Gloucester, the only surviving brother of Henry V, and the "Lord Protector," the power behind the throne when Henry VI was too young to rule.

*Gloucester, slandered and discredited, is called to a Parliament, where he is attacked in the middle of the night, probably by Suffolk, who --yes-- **suffocates** him, and emerges the next morning, reporting that Gloucester has died in his sleep.*

Even the credulous King Henry refuses to believe this story, and sentences Suffolk into exile for the murder of Gloucester.

The furious wailing of Queen Margaret reveals to anyone who cares to notice, that she and Suffolk have been having an affair.

As he is being deported, Suffolk's ship is boarded by pirates, who chop off his head, and ship it back to London.

Meanwhile, York decides that it is time to test the waters for an Yorkist takeover. He engages a belligerent peasant, Jack Cade, as provocateur. Cade absurdly declares himself to be the lost son of Edmund Mortimer, of the same line through which York intends to claim the crown.

Anarchy reigns! Queen Margaret is discovered distractedly cradling Suffolk's severed head! London is overrun by Cade's peasant rebellion! And Cade, himself, sits in judgement over the Lord High Treasurer of England...

CADE

Thou hast most traitorously corrupted the youth of the realm in erecting a grammar school; ...thou hast caused printing to be used, and... it will be proved to thy face thou hast men about thee that talk of a noun and a verb, and such abominable words as no Christian ear can endure to hear. ...Away with him! The proudest peer in the realm shall not wear a head on his shoulders, unless he pay me tribute; there shall not a maid be married, but she shall pay to me her maidenhead ere they have it: men shall hold of me *in capite*; and we charge and command that their wives be as free as heart can wish or tongue can tell.

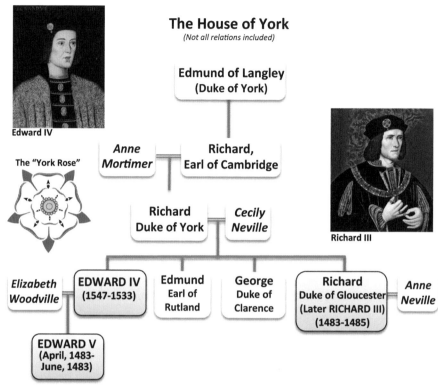

The House of York
(Not all relations included)

Edward IV

The "York Rose"

Edmund of Langley
(Duke of York)

Anne
Mortimer

Richard,
Earl of Cambridge

Richard
Duke of York

Cecily
Neville

Richard III

Elizabeth
Woodville

EDWARD IV
(1547-1533)

Edmund
Earl of
Rutland

George
Duke of
Clarence

Richard
Duke of Gloucester
(Later RICHARD III)
(1483-1485)

Anne
Neville

EDWARD V
(April, 1483-
June, 1483)

Margaret was not actually present at the Battle of Wakefield, where York and his son, Rutland, were killed. (She was in Scotland at the time, which makes this scene entirely Shakespeare's invention.) And, in fact, it was York who was killed during the battle, while his son was killed in the aftermath. Even so, Margaret was not innocent of the sort of cruelty that Shakespeare describes. Following the Second Battle of St. Albans, Margaret had the heads of two Yorkist knights chopped off, whose only job had been to see to it that Henry (her husband) came to no harm.

> How ill-beseeming is it in thy sex
> To triumph, like an Amazonian trull,
> Upon their woes whom fortune captivates!
> ...I would assay, proud queen, to make thee blush.
> To tell thee whence thou camest, of whom derived,
> Were shame enough to shame thee, wert thou not shameless...
> 'Tis beauty that doth oft make women proud;
> But, God he knows, thy share thereof is small:
> 'Tis virtue that doth make them most admired;
> The contrary doth make thee wonder'd at:
> 'Tis government that makes them seem divine;
> The want thereof makes thee abominable:
> Thou art as opposite to every good
> As the Antipodes are unto us,

The third Part of Henry the Sixt

(1455-1471)

Henry VI, Part Three picks up the action around 1455, with the peasant rebellion now safely quelled, but with many of the English lords now in full revolt. York briefly sets himself upon the throne, but is convinced to descend by Henry, who promises that the monarchy will pass to the line of York after his own death, effectively disinheriting his own son, Prince Edward.

*Queen Margaret is furious! She gathers up an army, along with the Lord Clifford, to attack the York faction, killing one of York's sons, and capturing York, himself. Before killing him, however, she taunts him: placing a paper crown upon his head, and forcing him to dry his tears with a handkerchief drenched in his own son's blood. This is generally considered to be **bad form**... And the portrait that Shakespeare paints of her brands her for all time as a villain, as York declares:*

YORK
She-wolf of France, but worse than wolves of France,
Whose tongue more poisons than the adder's tooth!
...O tiger's heart wrapt in a woman's hide!
How couldst thou drain the life-blood of the child,
To bid the father wipe his eyes withal,
And yet be seen to bear a woman's face?
...Keep thou the napkin, and go boast of this:
And if thou tell'st the heavy story right,
Upon my soul, the hearers will shed tears;
...Take me from the world:
My soul to heaven, my blood upon your heads!

Events and Major Battles of the War of the Roses
Shakespeare consolidates several of the battles, and even those few clashes depicted are only glancingly acknowledged in these pages. Here is a quick overview of the historical actions of the Lancastrians (Henry's side) and the Yorkists...

First Battle of Albans *(1455): Somerset is killed; Henry VI is captured by Earl of Warwick ("The Kingmaker") and York is made the "Lord Protector."*

Battle of Ludford Bridge *(1459): A troop of York's soldiers defect to the Lancaster side, and York and Warwick abandon their armies, fleeing to Ireland and Calais, respectively.*

Battle of Northampton *(1460): Though outnumbered, Warwick bribes Lord Grey (of the Lancaster side) to lay down his arms, letting the York army overrun the Lancastrians and capture King Henry again.*

Act of Accord *(1460): York arrives in London prepared to assume the throne, but his allies are unwilling to support his crowning. The House of Lords passes the Act of Accord, which establishes York as Lord Protector and pledges the monarchy to the line of York after Henry's death.*

Battle of Wakefield *(1460): York miscalculates either the size or position of the Lancastrian forces and he and his son, Rutland, are both killed.*

Second Battle of St. Albans *(1460): Edward is delayed by the* **Battle of Mortimer's Cross***, which enabled Margaret to defeat Warwick, regaining control of Henry VI (found after the battle sitting under a tree, singing), but the Londoners refuse to open their gates to Margaret's pillaging Lancastrian troops. When Edward finally arrives, he is welcomed in and crowned King Edward IV. (John Grey of Groby dies in this battle, and his widow, Elizabeth Woodville, becomes Edward's queen.)*

Battle of Towton *(1461): "Probably the largest and bloodiest battle ever fought on English soil," with perhaps 100,000 men participating and 28,000 killed amid a snowstorm. Henry flees to Scotland and Edward's right to rule is reinforced.*

Edward's Marriage *(1464) to Elizabeth Woodville results in special favors to her family, over the family of the Earl of Warwick ("the Nevilles"). Warwick switches sides to support Edward's brother, George, Duke of Clarence, and Edward flees to Burgundy (1470-71), enabling Henry to return briefly to the throne.*

Battle of Barnet *(April, 1471): Edward leads an army back into England, convincing his brother George to betray Warwick and rejoin them. Bad weather delays Margaret's return to England to support Warwick's forces. Amidst the fog, Warwick's Lancastrian forces mistake each other for Yorkists, and are killed by "friendly fire," leading to confusion and disruption among the Lancastrians. Edward recaptures King Henry and Warwick is killed in the midst of a retreat.*

Battle of Tewkesbury *(May, 1471): Margaret returns to England (too late to save Warwick); Prince Edward is killed, even as he begs the "perjured" George of Clarence (with whom he had been briefly allied), for mercy. The remaining Somerset brothers are killed, almost wiping out the remaining "Red Rose" side.*

And so, Margaret has his head chopped off... and set upon a pike... outside the gates of York... right next to that of his own son.

The remaining sons of York: Edward, the eldest, George, the Duke of Clarence, and Richard, "the hunchback," gather their forces to attack Margaret.

Shakespeare never directly informs us that the now-38-year-old Henry has begun showing signs of his late French grandfather's madness, but he certainly seems a bit "off." Of no use to anyone in battle, King Henry observes the horrific proceedings from a nearby hill:

KING HENRY VI

This battle fares like to the morning's war,
When dying clouds contend with growing light,
...Now sways it this way, like a mighty sea
Forced by the tide to combat with the wind;
Now sways it that way, like the selfsame sea
Forced to retire by fury of the wind:
Sometime the flood prevails, and then the wind;
Now one the better, then another best.
...Here on this molehill will I sit me down.
To whom God will, there be the victory!
For Margaret my queen, and Clifford too,
Have chid me from the battle; swearing both
They prosper best of all when I am thence.
Would I were dead! if God's good will were so;
For what is in this world but grief and woe?
O God! methinks it were a happy life,
To be no better than a homely swain;
To sit upon a hill, as I do now,
...Thereby to see the minutes how they run,
How many make the hour full complete;
How many hours bring about the day;
How many days will finish up the year;
How many years a mortal man may live.
When this is known, then to divide the times:
So many hours must I tend my flock;
So many hours must I take my rest;
So many hours must I contemplate;
So many hours must I sport myself;
...So minutes, hours, days, months, and years,
Pass'd over to the end they were created,
Would bring white hairs unto a quiet grave.

This is the longest soliloquy in all of Shakespeare, well worth piecing together to study at full length...

Ay, Edward will use women honourably.
Would he were wasted, marrow, bones and all,
That from his loins no hopeful branch may spring,
To cross me from the golden time I look for!
And yet, between my soul's desire and me--
The lustful Edward's title buried--
Is Clarence, Henry, and his son young Edward,
And all the unlook'd for issue of their bodies,
To take their rooms, ere I can place myself:
A cold premeditation for my purpose!
Why, then, I do but dream on sovereignty;
Like one that stands upon a promontory,
And spies a far-off shore where he would tread,
Wishing his foot were equal with his eye,
And chides the sea that sunders him from thence,
Saying, he'll lade it dry to have his way:
So do I wish the crown, being so far off;
And so I chide the means that keeps me from it;
And so I say, I'll cut the causes off,
Flattering me with impossibilities.
My eye's too quick, my heart o'erweens too much,
Unless my hand and strength could equal them.

And, for I should not deal in her soft laws,
She did corrupt frail nature with some bribe,
To shrink mine arm up like a wither'd shrub;
To make an envious mountain on my back,
Where sits deformity to mock my body;
To shape my legs of an unequal size;

And yet I know not how to get the crown,
For many lives stand between me and home:
And I,--like one lost in a thorny wood,
That rends the thorns and is rent with the thorns,
Seeking a way and straying from the way;
Not knowing how to find the open air,
But toiling desperately to find it out,--
Torment myself to catch the English crown:
And from that torment I will free myself,
Or hew my way out with a bloody axe.

This series of battles, which leave tens of thousands lying dead in their wake, thus fulfilling the prophecy of the Bishop of Carlisle that "the blood of English shall manure the ground," are ultimately won by the York brothers, and Edward assumes the throne as King Edward IV.

Edward immediately sets plans in motion for a politically advantageous marriage to a French princess... plans that are put on hold when a beautiful widow, Elizabeth Woodville (whose husband died in the recent battles), comes to court to petition for her late husband's estate. Edward, failing to seduce Elizabeth outright, offers to marry her instead, thus alienating the ambassador he'd sent to arrange the marriage to the French princess, the French Princess... and the French! Edward's envious brother, Richard, dreads the offspring that may spring from this unfortunate marriage, which will make his own path to the crown seemingly impossible.

GLOUCESTER (Richard)
...Well, say there is no kingdom then for Richard;
What other pleasure can the world afford?
I'll make my heaven in a lady's lap,
And deck my body in gay ornaments,
And witch sweet ladies with my words and looks.
O miserable thought! and more unlikely
Than to accomplish twenty golden crowns!
Why, love forswore me in my mother's womb:
...To disproportion me in every part,
Like to a chaos, or an unlick'd bear-whelp
That carries no impression like the dam.
And am I then a man to be beloved?
O monstrous fault, to harbour such a thought!
Then, since this earth affords no joy to me,
But to command, to cheque, to o'erbear such
As are of better person than myself,
I'll make my heaven to dream upon the crown,
And, whiles I live, to account this world but hell,
Until my mis-shaped trunk that bears this head
Be round impaled with a glorious crown.
...Why, I can smile, and murder whiles I smile,
And cry 'Content' to that which grieves my heart,
And wet my cheeks with artificial tears,
And frame my face to all occasions.
...I can add colours to the chameleon,
Change shapes with Proteus for advantages,

Richard III

In 1514, Thomas More, writing "A History of Richard III," catering to the Tudor anti-York bias, described Richard as "of body greatly deformed, the one shoulder higher than the other." The reputation of Richard-as-hunchback (see portrait at left, pointedly **not** deformed) is not supported by historical record or contemporary reports. Shakespeare takes More's vague rumor of "deformity" to create a hunchbacked, club-footed, shriveled-arm monster, wretched in body, mind and spirit. Of course, it is Shakespeare's astonishingly vivid depiction of evil that the world remembers.

In addition to the French, Margaret has now joined with the Earl of Warwick (who had been King Edward's ambassador to arrange the marriage to the French Princess). The political nuances of the French position are complicated, given that the French, themselves, have their own civil divides: the Burgundians having sided with King Edward while the French monarchy sides with Margaret.

Following Edward's death, Queen Margaret ultimately finds herself living in exile in France. This contrasts with Shakespeare's depiction of her in **Richard III**, which features her lingering in England, engaging in ironic conversations with the other queens: Queen Elizabeth (widow of King Edward), Queen Anne (wife of Richard, though we never see her after her coronation), and the Duchess of York (mother to Edward, George and Richard: she is essentially the "Queen Mum.") This proliferation of queens, like the multiple Edwards, Richards, Henrys, or Elizabeths can be confusing. (It is, of course, easier to follow when seeing it live on stage.)

Clarence's "perjury" features him swearing allegiance to his brother Edward, then to the Earl of Warwick, and once again to his brother Edward. He would obviously resent having this pointed out, much as Richard dislikes having his deformities mocked, or as Edward hates allusions to his voracious sexual appetite.

While Shakespeare clearly has chosen Richard as his villain, in real life, one might have made as strong a case for George, who repeatedly acts in bad faith.

King Henry has waited through three long plays to take any kind of strong, self-directed action. Even his decision to exile Suffolk was heavily influenced by public riots protesting Suffolk's presence. (Suffolk was not, in reality, exiled for the murder of Gloucester, but for suspicion of treason.) But here, for once, Henry insults Richard out of his own ill-timed impulsive peevishness.

GLOUCESTER (Richard) *(Continued)*
And set the murderous Machiavel to school.
Can I do this, and cannot get a crown?
Tut, were it farther off, I'll pluck it down.

*Margaret joins forces with the alienated French to attack King Edward, but this time finds herself captured along with her son, the **other** Edward in the play, **Prince** Edward. Prince Edward, who will not live to see his eighteenth birthday, defies the York brothers, sneering…*

PRINCE EDWARD
I know my duty; you are all undutiful:
Lascivious Edward, and thou perjured George,
And thou mis-shapen Dick, I tell ye all
I am your better, traitors as ye are:
And thou usurp'st my father's right and mine.

King Edward takes revenge for Margaret's heartless killing of his father: stabbing Prince Edward while she watches helplessly…

KING EDWARD IV
Take that, thou likeness of this railer here.
                              (Stabs him)
Richard cannot resist getting in on the fun…

GLOUCESTER (Richard)
Sprawl'st thou? take that, to end thy agony.
                              (Stabs him)
And then George, the Duke of Clarence, perhaps out of peer pressure…

CLARENCE (George)
And there's for twitting me with perjury.
                              (Stabs him)
Richard rushes back to London, finding Henry, who is being held captive in the tower. Even the pious Henry cannot resist scorning Richard as…

KING HENRY VI
…an indigested and deformed lump,
…Teeth hadst thou in thy head when thou wast born,
To signify thou camest to bite the world:

And so, Richard kills him.

The adaptation of this particular monologue is the result of extreme slicing and dicing... Here it is in full, below...

Richard III

RICHARD (GLOUCESTER)
(Now is the winter of our discontent
Made glorious summer by this sun of York;)
And all the clouds that lour'd upon our house
In the deep bosom of the ocean buried.
Now are our brows bound with victorious wreaths;
Our bruised arms hung up for monuments;
Our stern alarums changed to merry meetings,
Our dreadful marches to delightful measures.
(Grim-visaged war hath smooth'd his wrinkled front;)
And now, instead of mounting barded steeds
To fright the souls of fearful adversaries,
(He capers nimbly in a lady's chamber
To the lascivious pleasing of a lute.
But I, that am not shaped for sportive tricks,)
Nor made to court an amorous looking-glass;
I, that am rudely stamp'd, and want love's majesty
To strut before a wanton ambling nymph;
I, that am curtail'd of this fair proportion,
Cheated of feature by dissembling nature,
Deformed, unfinish'd, sent before my time
Into this breathing world, scarce half made up,
And that so lamely and unfashionable
That dogs bark at me as I halt by them;
Why, I, in this weak piping time of peace,
Have no delight to pass away the time,
Unless to spy my shadow in the sun
And descant on mine own deformity:
And therefore, (since I cannot prove a lover,)
To entertain these fair well-spoken days,
(I am determined to prove a villain)
And hate the idle pleasures of these days.
(Plots have I laid, inductions dangerous,
By drunken prophecies, libels and dreams,
To set my brother Clarence and the king
In deadly hate the one against the other:)
And if King Edward be as true and just
As I am subtle, false and treacherous,
This day should Clarence closely be mew'd up,
About a prophecy, which says that 'G'
Of Edward's heirs the murderer shall be.
Dive, thoughts, down to my soul: here
Clarence comes.

The Tragedy of Richard the Third

(1471-1485)

With Henry and Prince Edward now both safely assassinated, peace breaks out, and Richard begins making plans to elbow his brothers out of the way.

RICHARD (GLOUCESTER)
Now is the winter of our discontent
Made glorious summer by this sun of York
...Grim-visaged war hath smooth'd his wrinkled front;
And... capers nimbly in a lady's chamber
To the lascivious pleasing of a lute.
But I, that am not shaped for sportive tricks,
I, that am rudely stamp'd, and want love's majesty...
Deformed, unfinish'd, sent before my time
Into this breathing world, scarce half made up,
...Since I cannot prove a lover,
I am determined to prove a villain:
Plots have I laid, inductions dangerous,
By drunken prophecies, libels and dreams,
To set my brother Clarence and the king
In deadly hate the one against the other.

Lady Anne, the widow of the late Prince Edward, is discovered following the corpse of her Father-in Law, Henry VI...

LADY ANNE
Cursed be the hand that made these fatal holes!
Cursed be the heart that had the heart to do it!
Cursed the blood that let this blood from hence!
...If ever he have wife, let her be made
As miserable by the death of him
As I am made by my poor lord and thee!

This speech by Anne (previous page) is more ironic than it is predictive... one of the very few curses/predictions that does NOT come true in a Shakespeare History play (given that Richard outlives her). To be fair, later, Anne will also suggest, "Annointed let me be with deadly venom, / And die, ere men can say, God save the queen." (which is probably closer to the end result).

Richard III

I'll have her; but I will not keep her long.
What! I, that kill'd her husband and his father,
To take her in her heart's extremest hate,
With curses in her mouth, tears in her eyes,
The bleeding witness of her hatred by;
Having God, her conscience, and these bars against me,
And I nothing to back my suit at all,
But the plain devil and dissembling looks,
And yet to win her, all the world to nothing!
Ha!

A sweeter and a lovelier gentleman,
Framed in the prodigality of nature,
Young, valiant, wise, and, no doubt, right royal,
The spacious world cannot again afford
And will she yet debase her eyes on me,
That cropp'd the golden prime of this sweet prince,
And made her widow to a woful bed?
On me, whose all not equals Edward's moiety?
On me, that halt and am unshapen thus?
My dukedom to a beggarly denier,

Go, after, after, cousin Buckingham.
The mayor towards Guildhall hies him in all post:
There, at your meet'st advantage of the time,
(Infer the bastardy of Edward's children:)
Tell them how Edward put to death a citizen,
Only for saying he would make his son
Heir to the crown; meaning indeed his house,
Which, by the sign thereof was termed so.

...Even where his lustful eye or savage heart,
Without control, listed to make his prey.

58

Little does Anne realize that she has actually been cursing herself! For, in a moment, Richard will arrive and audaciously attempt to seduce the widow of the man that he, himself, killed! And she, astonishingly, begins to fall for his seduction! This is doubly ironic, given the fact that Richard only began his murderous rampage out of the certainty that no woman could ever possibly love him.

RICHARD (GLOUCESTER)

Was ever woman in this humour woo'd?
Was ever woman in this humour won?
...Hath she forgot already that brave prince,
Edward, her lord, whom I, some three months since,
Stabb'd in my angry mood at Tewksbury?
...I do mistake my person all this while:
Upon my life, she finds, although I cannot,
Myself to be a marvellous proper man.
I'll be at charges for a looking-glass,
And entertain some score or two of tailors,
To study fashions to adorn my body:
Since I am crept in favour with myself,
I will maintain it with some little cost.
But first I'll turn yon fellow in his grave;
And then return lamenting to my love.
Shine out, fair sun, till I have bought a glass,
That I may see my shadow as I pass.
Exit

Richard conspires to frame his brother, George, to look like a traitor to his brother Edward, the King, who reluctantly has George confined in the tower, where one of Richard's henchmen stabs him, and drowns him in a butt of wine! King Edward, racked with guilt and remorse over George's death, dies not long thereafter, and Richard begins a secret, relentless campaign to be made King, going so far as to smear the reputation of his own nephews.

RICHARD (GLOUCESTER)

Infer the bastardy of Edward's children:
...Moreover, urge his hateful luxury
And bestial appetite in change of lust;
Which stretched to their servants, daughters, wives...
Nay, for a need, thus far come near my person:
Tell them, when that my mother went with child

Lady Anne seems to have spent most of her marriage in misery, brooding: "For never yet one hour in his bed / Have I enjoyed the golden dew of sleep." Muttering that Richard "hates me for my father Warwick," Anne predicts that he "will, no doubt, shortly be rid of me." A couple of scenes later, Richard barely mentions, "And Anne my wife hath bid the world good night."

Richard III

Look, what is done cannot be now amended:
Men shall deal unadvisedly sometimes,
Which after hours give leisure to repent.
(If I did take the kingdom from your sons,
To make amends, Ill give it to your daughter.)
If I have kill'd the issue of your womb,
To quicken your increase, I will beget
Mine issue of your blood upon your daughter
A grandam's name is little less in love
Than is the doting title of a mother;
They are as children but one step below,
Even of your mettle, of your very blood;
Of an one pain, save for a night of groans
Endured of her, for whom you bid like sorrow.

I cannot make you what amends I would,
Therefore accept such kindness as I can.
Dorset your son, that with a fearful soul
Leads discontented steps in foreign soil,
This fair alliance quickly shall call home
To high promotions and great dignity:
The king, that calls your beauteous daughter wife.
Familiarly shall call thy Dorset brother;
(Again shall you be mother to a king,)
And all the ruins of distressful times
Repair'd with double riches of content.
What! we have many goodly days to see:
The liquid drops of tears that you have shed
Shall come again, transform'd to orient pearl,
Advantaging their loan with interest
Of ten times double gain of happiness.

Prepare her ears to hear a wooer's tale
Put in her tender heart the aspiring flame
Of golden sovereignty; (acquaint the princess
With the sweet silent hours of marriage joys)
And when this arm of mine hath chastised
The petty rebel, dull-brain'd Buckingham,
(Bound with triumphant garlands will I come
And lead thy daughter to a conqueror's bed;)
To whom I will retail my conquest won,
And she shall be sole victress, Caesar's Caesar.

RICHARD (GLOUCESTER) *(Continued)*
Of that unsatiate Edward, noble York
My princely father then had wars in France
And, by just computation of the time,
Found that the issue was not his begot;
Which well appeared in his lineaments,
Being nothing like the noble duke my father:
But touch this sparingly, as 'twere far off,
Because you know, my lord, my mother lives.

*The late King Edward's eldest son is briefly crowned King Edward V, and Richard has both of Edward's sons conveyed to the Tower, supposedly for their protection, but where they, too, are (you can probably say it with me by now) "**assassinated**." He strategizes to replace Lady Anne (who has probably been poisoned at this point) with a new bride who will lend greater weight of succession to his fledgling monarchy.*

He chooses Elizabeth of York, the daughter of his brother, Edward, and sister to the two boys he had killed in the tower. He explains this great idea to the girl's mother, Edward's widow, Queen Elizabeth.

KING RICHARD III
If I did take the kingdom from your sons,
To make amends, I'll give it to your daughter.
…Your children were vexation to your youth,
But mine shall be a comfort to your age.
The loss you have is but a son being king,
And by that loss your daughter is made queen.
…Again shall you be mother to a king.
…Go, then my mother, to thy daughter go
Make bold her bashful years with your experience;
…Acquaint the princess
With the sweet silent hours of marriage joys
Bound with triumphant garlands will I come
And lead thy daughter to a conqueror's bed.

QUEEN ELIZABETH replies:
What were I best to say? her father's brother
Would be her lord? or shall I say, her uncle?
Or, he that slew her brothers and her uncles?
Under what title shall I woo for thee,
That God, the law, my honour and her love,
Can make seem pleasing to her tender years?

Descendants of John of Gaunt
(Not all relations included)

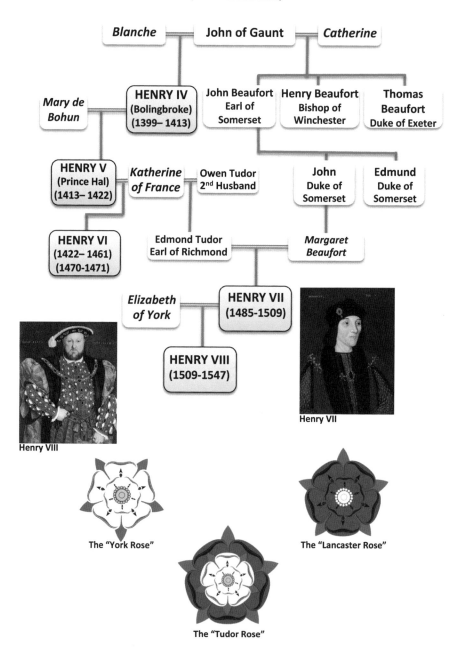

Blanche ——— John of Gaunt ——— Catherine

Mary de Bohun

HENRY IV
(Bolingbroke)
(1399– 1413)

John Beaufort
Earl of
Somerset

Henry Beaufort
Bishop of
Winchester

Thomas
Beaufort
Duke of Exeter

HENRY V
(Prince Hal)
(1413– 1422)

*Katherine
of France*

Owen Tudor
2nd Husband

John
Duke of
Somerset

Edmund
Duke of
Somerset

HENRY VI
(1422– 1461)
(1470-1471)

Edmond Tudor
Earl of Richmond

*Margaret
Beaufort*

*Elizabeth
of York*

HENRY VII
(1485-1509)

HENRY VIII
(1509-1547)

Henry VII

Henry VIII

The "York Rose"

The "Lancaster Rose"

The "Tudor Rose"

62

Queen Elizabeth quietly smuggles young Elizabeth out of the country, bringing her to join the forces of Henry Tudor, the Earl of Richmond.

Henry is actually the grandson of... **Somerset!** *(...Who we may remember was the legitimized bastard grandson of John of Gaunt, the fourth son of Edward III, by way of Gaunt's eventual third wife.)*

He is, essentially, the only surviving heir of the "**Red Rose**" *side of the War of the Roses, and will ultimately become* **King Henry VII,** *marrying his own Red Rose side with the White Rose by way of Elizabeth of York, thus creating the Tudor line of English kings and finally concluding the War of the Roses!*

But first, Henry must raise an army to attack Richard, whose forces either fall, switch sides or desert the battlefield. Richard's own horse is cut out from under him and, refusing to withdraw, he is left crying out...

KING RICHARD III
I have set my life upon a cast,
And I will stand the hazard of the die:
...A horse! a horse! my kingdom for a horse!

The Formation of the House of Tudor
(Not all relations included)

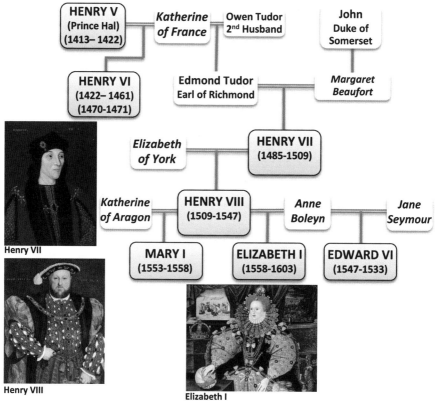

Henry VII

Henry VIII

Elizabeth I

The Tudor line actually reaches back almost to King Henry V, as, following Henry's death, Katherine of France remarried, this time to Owen Tudor. This connects the bloodline of Henry VII, Henry VIII and Elizabeth I to Henry VI, as well as "King Charles the Mad," by way of Katherine.

This easily-overlooked connection is the prime reason that Shakespeare (and probably anyone else who wanted to remain in the good graces of Queen Elizabeth) would soft-pedal any references to the French King as "King Charles the Mad," or any similar hints that Henry VI suffered his own bouts of madness.

Conversely, this is also probably the reason that characters who are not directly blood-related to Elizabeth (such as Queen Margaret) or who directly opposed the Tudor line (such as Richard III), are made scapegoats and villains.

And while modern audiences likely see this speech of Henry VIII as a clumsy ploy to drop his wife in favor of his mistress, for Shakespeare to make that case (knowing that the second marriage found its fruition in their current queen) would be extremely risky. As these many plays make clear, the lack of a male heir does, indeed, put Henry's realms in "danger," and, after all that England had been through, Shakespeare's audience knew it.

The Famous History of the Life of King HENRY the Eight.

(1520-1533)

*Shakespeare skips ahead 35 years into the monarchy of Henry VIII. Written in collaboration with John Fletcher, **Henry VIII** finds Henry's first wife, Katherine, failing to give birth to a son, giving Henry (who has conveniently fallen in love with Anne Boleyn in the meantime) the opportunity to petition for an annulment.*

Henry argues that his lack of a male heir is God's punishment for having married the widow of his brother. Despite all insistence that the Spanish Princess Katherine, a teenage bride at the time, had never consummated this previous relationship, Henry contends in court...

KING HENRY VIII
Methought I stood not in the smile of heaven;
              ...for her male issue
Or died where they were made, or shortly after:
              ...hence I took a thought,
This was a judgment on me;
I weigh'd the danger which my realms stood in
By this my issue's fail... Thus hulling in
The wild sea of my conscience, I did steer
Toward this remedy, whereupon we are
Now present here together.

The powerful Cardinal Wolsey, dispatched by Henry to argue his case to the Pope, is discovered playing a double game, secretly siding with Rome while amassing funds from the treasury to support his own bid to become Pope. And while the authorship of many of the speeches in **Henry VIII** *may be suspect, this speech from Wolsey, contemplating the secondary nature of power that is derived from the king, is clearly Shakespeare's contribution.*

Moments before this speech, Henry has left Wolsey with a packet of intercepted papers, storming off.

CARDINAL WOOLSEY

This paper has undone me: 'tis the account
Of all that world of wealth I have drawn together
For mine own ends; indeed, to gain the popedom,
And fee my friends in Rome. O negligence!
Fit for a fool to fall by: what cross devil
Made me put this main secret in the packet
I sent the king? Is there no way to cure this?
No new device to beat this from his brains?
I know 'twill stir him strongly; yet I know
A way, if it take right, in spite of fortune
Will bring me off again. What's this? 'To the Pope!'
The letter, as I live, with all the business
I writ to's holiness. Nay then, farewell!
I have touch'd the highest point of all my greatness;
And, from that full meridian of my glory,
I haste now to my setting: I shall fall
Like a bright exhalation in the evening,
And no man see me more. ...I have ventured,
Like little wanton boys that swim on bladders,
This many summers in a sea of glory,
But far beyond my depth... O, how wretched
Is that poor man that hangs on princes' favours!
There is, betwixt that smile we would aspire to,
That sweet aspect of princes, and their ruin,
More pangs and fears than wars or women have:
And when he falls, he falls like Lucifer,
Never to hope again.

Let me speak, sir,
For heaven now bids me; and the words I utter
Let none think flattery, for they'll find 'em truth...

This final speech was almost certainly written by Fletcher, but the very clumsiness with which Cranmer expresses this obsequious flattery fittingly climaxes the themes that saturate the ten plays leading up to this final coda (even if we cannot help but seeing it with more jaded amusement than was probably intended).

The church, not wanting to offend Katherine's home country, the very powerful, Catholic and rich nation of Spain, refuses to grant the annulment. Henry marries Anne Boleyn anyway, thus earning an excommunication from the church, to which he retaliates by breaking off the Church of England from the Roman Catholic Church, thus launching the English Reformation.

Given that the King theoretically rules by Divine Right, changing one's religious orientation in the midst of one's monarchy can be a dicey affair, and destabilize a kingship, which becomes dependent upon burnings and beheadings for a time.

*Eventually, Anne Boleyn gives birth to... **a girl! Elizabeth**, who will rule over most of Shakespeare's career as Queen Elizabeth I, a period not-so-coincidentally known as the "Elizabethan Era."*

Shakespeare (or, perhaps, Fletcher) places a wild prophecy into the mouth of Cranmer, the Archbishop of Canterbury, who, in the most pandering, politically calibrated speech in all of Shakespeare (or, maybe, Fletcher), presides over Elizabeth's christening, boldly prophesying:

CRANMER
...This royal infant--heaven still move about her!--
Though in her cradle, yet now promises
Upon this land a thousand thousand blessings,
Which time shall bring to ripeness: she shall be
A pattern to all princes living with her,
And all that shall succeed: ...all princely graces,
That mould up such a mighty piece as this is,
With all the virtues that attend the good,
Shall still be doubled on her: truth shall nurse her,
Holy and heavenly thoughts still counsel her:
She shall be loved and fear'd: her own shall bless her;
Her foes shake like a field of beaten corn,
And hang their heads with sorrow: good grows with her:
In her days every man shall eat in safety,
Under his own vine, what he plants; and sing
The merry songs of peace to all his neighbours:
God shall be truly known; and those about her
From her shall read the perfect ways of honour,
And by those claim their greatness, not by blood.

Nor shall this peace sleep with her: but as when
The bird of wonder dies, the maiden phoenix,
Her ashes new create another heir,
As great in admiration as herself;
So shall she leave her blessedness to one,
When heaven shall call her from this cloud of darkness,
Who from the sacred ashes of her honour
Shall star-like rise, as great in fame as she was,
And so stand fix'd: peace, plenty, love, truth, terror,
That were the servants to this chosen infant,
Shall then be his, and like a vine grow to him:
Wherever the bright sun of heaven shall shine,
His honour and the greatness of his name
Shall be, and make new nations: he shall flourish,
And, like a mountain cedar, reach his branches
To all the plains about him: our children's children
Shall see this, and bless heaven.

KING HENRY
Thou speakest wonders...

As we reach the climax of this tale, Shakespeare (or Fletcher) reaches past the monarchy of Queen Elizabeth, to simultaneously puff up the rule of James I, who followed Elizabeth. It is quite possible that this passage (above) was added after the 1603 death of Queen Elizabeth as a paean to the new king.

Whatever the likely impulse behind the inclusion of King James in this play, introducing a new character on the final page is generally an unwelcome surprise, and keeping our scope confined to Elizabeth, whose influence can be felt throughout these works (name-checked on the first page of this adaptation), is probably the best way to go.

Elizabeth I

James I

CRANMER *(Continued)*
...She shall be, to the happiness of England,
An aged princess; many days shall see her,
And yet no day without a deed to crown it.
Would I had known no more! but she must die,
She must, the saints must have her; yet a virgin,
A most unspotted lily shall she pass
To the ground, and all the world shall mourn her.

And so it was.

The history of England, from 1066 to 1533, as told by our most profound, though not necessarily our most reliable narrator of the time.

I now pronounce you all thoroughly inducted into the lore of Shakespeare's Histories. Unfortunately for me I had to leave lots of great stuff on the cutting room floor in order to get it all in. The great news for you is that it's all still out there, waiting for you to discover, and now you know all you need to know, to know the rest!

PICTURE SOURCES[8]

NATIONAL PORTRAIT GALLERY
Edward III (p. 12, 20, 38), Edward IV (pgs. 48), Henry I (p.4), Henry II, (pgs. 4, 6), Henry IV (pgs. 12, 18, 20, 22, 26), Henry V (pgs. 20, 22, 28, 30), Henry VI (pgs. 38, 40), Henry VII (pgs. 62, 64), King John (p. 6, 8), Richard II (pgs. 12, 14, 16, 18, 20), Richard III (pgs. 48, 56, 58, 60), William the Conqueror (p. 4)

WILSON, DEREK, THE PLANTAGENET CHRONICLES; 1154-1485, METRO BOOKS, NY, 2011
Edward I, from the collection of Lee Hutchinson (p. 12), Henry III, from the collection of the Bridgeman Art Library (p. 12)

LEE RUSHTON
Angevin Empire, (p. 4), Angevin Empire After John (p. 10), Henry's Interrupted Path (p. 34)

WIKIMEDIA COMMONS
James I by Paulus van Somer, from the collection of the Museo Nacional del Prado (p. 68)

WIKIPEDIA
Elizabeth I, Attributed to George Gower, from the collection of the Woburn Abbey (pgs. 64, 68), Joan of Arc, from the Centre Historique des Archives Nationales (p. 42), The "Lancaster Rose" (pgs. 40, 62), The "Tudor Rose" (p. 62), The "York Rose" (pgs. 38, 48, 62)

THE-ATHENAEUM.ORG
Henry VIII, by Hans Holbein the Younger, 1540, from the collection of Galleria Nazionale di Arte Antica, Rome (pgs. 62, 64)

FOLGER SHAKESPEARE LIBRARY
First Folio Play Titles (King John, p. 7; Richard II, p. 13; Henry IV, Part 1, p. 21; Henry IV, Part 2, p. 27; Henry V, p. 31; Henry VI, Part 1, p. 39; Henry VI, Part 2, p. 45; Henry VI, Part 3, p. 49; Richard III, p. 57; Henry VIII, p. 65)

---

[8] Images of the English Kings, and the First Folio Edition, produced in the 15th, 16th & 17th centuries, and the Lancaster, Tudor and York Roses are in the public domain. Maps are the original creation of Lee Rushton, © 2014.

Also available from TMRT Press…
Molière Than Thou

Best of Fringe: Best Adapted Work. *San Francisco Fringe Festival*

The audience is enthralled… Timothy Mooney is the real deal… A very tight performance indeed, which should be seen by any aspiring actor who wants to tread the boards. *George Psillidies, nytheatre.com*

"Top Ten of 2006" One-of-a-kind… original, weird and seriously funny… one of the most creative and refreshing pieces of classical theatre I've seen in years… Mooney's translations make Molière's 17th century language instantly accessible. His interpretations were crisp, stylized and sang with the comic genius of the playwright's original intent. *Ruth Cartlidge, Chattanooga Pulse*

Mooney is clearly enraptured by the great French playwright… The translations are wonderful… well worth seeing. *Amy Barratt, Montreal Mirror*

The humanities are in safe hands this year. *San Francisco Bay Guardian*

Molière has never been more accessible… *Marie J. Kilker, aislesay.com*

Outstanding… A number of patrons found the performance too short, because they could have listened to Mr. Mooney all day. *Ken Gordon, CBC*

The listener can draw all the available pleasure from the splendid speeches penned by the man considered the French Shakespeare.
Kevin Prokosh, Winnipeg Free Press

Clearly Molière lives. *Elizabeth Maupin, Orlando Sentinel*

A must-see for aspiring drama students and a pleasant experience for the rest of us… *The Vue Weekly, Edmonton*

I highly recommend his skilled impersonation of one of the theater's most gifted and important creative spirits. *Al Krulik, Orlando Weekly*

If you're not passionate about Molière now, you may well be at the end of the show… *Marianne Hales Harding – Seattle Fringe Fest Review Rag*

One of the reasons that Molière's work has survived is that, sadly, his enemies have outlived him… But what he left us were his vast quantity of words… articulate, brilliant, hilarious, disgusting, despairing… *We need his voice. And he's funny as hell.* *Minnesota Fringe Blogger, Phillip Low*

TMRT Press, PO Box 638, Prospect Heights, IL 60070 * www.timmooneyrep.com

Also Available from TMRT Press!

CRITERIA
A One-Man, Comic, Sci-Fi Thriller!

An *engaging and brilliant* performance.   *Edmonton VueWeekly*

Provocative, funny, thoughtful, shocking and compelling. Stuff like this is what the fringe is all about. See it.   *Quentin Mills-Fenn, Winnipeg Uptown*

A sci-fi action flick, a thriller, a mystery and a road movie [with] a riveting *edge-of-your-seat finale.*   *Cheryl Binning, Winnipeg Free Press*

On his journey, the terrorist enters a diner where he encounters friendly small-town locals. His shock and horror at the decadence of a society where a waitress calls everyone "honey" *almost brought the house down...*
     Stacy Rowland, TheatreSeattle.com

It approaches politics more successfully than any other show... It's smart, it's nuanced -- and everybody needs to see it...   *Phillip Low, Fringe Blogger*

...Should be performed for corporate executives or at political gatherings and then discussed all night.   *George Savage, Playwright (On-line Review)*

"One Man Apocalypse!" "There's not a lot of optimism (though there's plenty of apocalypse-relieving comedy).   *Courtney McLean (On-line Review)*

The language in this play is *astonishing... pulling us along, off-balance and breathless with incomprehension...* If I laughed, it would have to have been the laugh of catastrophe: giddy with hopelessness... a really exciting evening of virtuoso theater.   *Richard Greene, Georgia College & State University*

A comic espionage sequence Woody Allen might have written. The drama unfolds at a captivating pace and the dark comedy crackles.
     Fringe Review Rag, Seattle 2003

The action is exciting, the consequences chilling and the story telling superb.
     Carl Gauze, Ink 19

Very compelling... *Hard to explain but easy to enjoy.*
     Bret Fetzer, The Stranger Weekly Magazine

A futuristic, sci-fi conspiracy thriller that *will have you on the edge of your seat...*   *Ken Gordon, The Jenny Revue*

TMRT Press, PO Box 638, Prospect Heights, IL 60070 * www.timmooneyrep.com

Also Available from TMRT Press!

The Big Book of Molière Monologues
Hilarious Performance Pieces From Our Greatest Comic Playwright

Molière's lines, penned in Classical French over three centuries ago found exuberant reaffirmation in Tim's smooth and stylish English translation… His book of monologues is a masterwork. *I've never seen a better compilation.*
    William Luce, Author, The Belle of Amherst, Barrymore, The Last Flapper

Offers more than the title would suggest. True, there are 160 or so of Molière monologues… But he also provides plot summaries and contextual information, as well as an introduction to the life and work of Molière, guides to the performance of classical verse monologues and stopwatch timings of each piece for audition purposes.   *Stage Directions Magazine*

A must-read for Molière's fans and neophytes… a riveting introduction to Molière and his work… incredibly faithful to the spirit of the plays. Mooney was able to put into verse even those works that had been originally written in prose and the effect is outstanding.   *Pascale-Anne Brault, DePaul University*

Mooney's exhaustive research, scholarship, and experience has made him one of the world's leading experts on Molière… invaluable to anyone interested in the "nuts and bolts" of 17th century French Comedy... My best advice: buy this book and then bring Mr. Mooney to your institution or venue to see him bring the book to life!   *Aaron Adair, Southeastern Oklahoma State University*

FANTASTIC! As an educator, reading it was akin to attending a master class. As a director, I am "chomping at the bit" to work on a Molière piece again.
    James McDonnell, Fine Arts Chair, College of the Sequoias

The perfect accompaniment to my study of Molière - a fabulous collection of some of Molière's most hilarious pieces written creatively for the current actor... This book can help you find the perfect monologue before you go searching through every single play out there.   *Sean B. (On-Line Review)*

An elegantly simplistic highway of understanding, from the basic description of iambs to the delivery of easily understood, and laughed out loud at, skillfully constructed verse… Tim's *Big Book* facilitates this in a very American, in your face way, like Mad Magazine or the old Saturday Night Live... You will be delighted, fulfilled and even a bit smarter in the timeless clever ingenuity of Molière and Mooney's genius manner of bringing this genre to life!   *John Paul Molière, Hume, Virginia*
    (Yes, that's right; my name is Molière, it's not a misprint.)

TMRT Press, PO Box 638, Prospect Heights, IL 60070 * www.timmooneyrep.com

Acting at the Speed of Life
Conquering Theatrical Style

A unique, refreshing and highly practical approach… No nonsense steps to approach the demands of stylized acting… This exceedingly valuable book will inspire actors to approach stylized theatre with the spirit of fun and style.
            James Fisher, Theatre Library Association's "Broadside"

Author Timothy Mooney takes on the challenges of asides, soliloquies and rhetorical speech. He offers tips on memorizing lines, incorporating the "stuff" of historical style, and going beyond naturalism and realism as it suits the playwright's intent. *Nicely done.*   *Stage Directions Magazine*

A gem of a book that demystifies the acting process by mixing common-sense instruction with practical exercises. It ought to have a place on every actor's and director's bookshelf. Not that it ought to stay there. Keep it handy for audition preparation, classroom studies, rehearsals and sometimes simply for a good read… He inspires his readers with a clear common-sense approach, eye-opening analyses of familiar texts, and wise advice that encourages newcomers and veteran actors to grow into the best they can be.
            Michael Howley, Southern Theatre

Terrific… Replete with incisive, clear-headed accessible advice… The clearest and most comprehensive work for the community and student actor written today.   *Dr. Christian H. Moe, Southern Illinois University*

Not just your average acting book: A comprehensive understanding of the basic skills needed to survive. Powerful and empowering… it's necessary for every serious actor's shelf.   *Dennis Wemm, Glenville State College*

The hardest-working book in my life of teaching acting to high school students… From the basics of memorization to the clearing of the cobwebs surrounding the classics, the book does it all with grace and great humor.
            Claudia Haas, Playwright for Youth/Artist in Residence, Twin Cities

A thunderous success! My cabaret class came alive with interpretive freedom.
            Loren F. Salter, Artistic Director and Performance Coach

Probably the most accessible approach to classical style that I have ever seen.
            Celi Oliveto, Master of Letters/MFA Candidate, Mary Baldwin College

This could be the modern manual for the Director and the Actor.
            Charley Ault, Director, Players Guild of the Festival Playhouse

NO other book I've read captures these simple tasks that are so important.
            Janice Fronczak, University of Nebraska-Kearney

TMRT Press, PO Box 638, Prospect Heights, IL 60070 * www.timmooneyrep.com

If you enjoyed this book…

- You may want to share it with friends, teach it in your classes, or get copies for your library…
- You may want to stage it with your students or theatre company…
- You may want to share your own reactions, thoughts and stories with the author…
- You may want to follow Tim's exploits, read his blog, or learn of other works available from TMRT Press, such as *Acting at the Speed of Life*, *Conquering Theatrical Style*, *The Big Book of Moliere Monologues*, *Moliere than Thou*, or *Criteria, a One-Man Sci-Fi Thriller!*

If so, please go to **www.timmooneyrep.com** for lots of fun stuff, including links to blog, video, scripts and bookings for *Shakespeare's Histories*, *Lot o' Shakespeare*, *Moliere than Thou* and *The Greatest Speech of All Time!*

Or, you can fill out the form below, and send it with your order for more copies of the book to:

TMRT Press
c/o Timothy Mooney
P.O. Box 638
Prospect Heights, IL 60070

You can also send your thoughts, comments and stories to this address. Tim loves reading your feedback, input and adventures!

Name _____

Address _____

City, State, Zip _____

Telephone _____

E-mail address _____

I would like to order ____ copies of "_____"!

I would like info for ordering multiple copies for school or library use! ❑

I would also like to be on the list for Tim's Blog! ❑

I would like to talk licensing this play for production! ❑

Other comments and thoughts (use additional pages, if necessary!):

_____

_____

_____

Thank you for your enthusiasm!
Tim Mooney

Made in the USA
Charleston, SC
10 January 2014